IN THE WAR

IN THE WAR

WOUNDED BUT WINNING

*Though at times hopelessness seems overwhelming,
this war can be won.*

BOB MCLAUGHLIN

XULON PRESS

Xulon Press
2301 Lucien Way #415
Maitland, FL 32751
407.339.4217
www.xulonpress.com

© 2022 by Bob McLaughlin

Contribution by: Trudy McLaughlin

All rights reserved solely by the author. The author guarantees all contents are original and do not infringe upon the legal rights of any other person or work. No part of this book may be reproduced in any form without the permission of the author.

Due to the changing nature of the Internet, if there are any web addresses, links, or URLs included in this manuscript, these may have been altered and may no longer be accessible. The views and opinions shared in this book belong solely to the author and do not necessarily reflect those of the publisher. The publisher therefore disclaims responsibility for the views or opinions expressed within the work.

Unless otherwise indicated, Scripture quotations taken from the King James Version (KJV)—*public domain.*

Scripture quotations taken from the New American Standard Bible (NASB). Copyright © 1960, 1962, 1963, 1968, 1971, 1972, 1973, 1975, 1977, 1995 by The Lockman Foundation. Used by permission. All rights reserved.

Paperback ISBN-13: 978-1-66286-478-0
Hard Cover ISBN-13: 978-1-66286-479-7
Ebook ISBN-13: 978-1-66286-480-3

Table of Contents

Dedication.. xi
About The Book xiii
Endorsements xv
Preface xvii
Introduction... xxiii

PART ONE: INTO THIS WAR 1

Chapter 1:   Please Don't Shoot 3
Chapter 2:   Get On The Floor and Lick That Up Like A Dog..... 7
Chapter 3:   He's Just Like His Father 13
Chapter 4:   When Do I Go Home? 19
Chapter 5:   I Hate This Life! 23
Chapter 6:   Searching For Acceptance 29

PART TWO: CONVERSION 33

Chapter 7:   Two Men Prayed and God Answered 35
Chapter 8:   A New Beginning 41
Chapter 9:   The Visitor................................... 49
Chapter 10: The Call 53
Chapter 11: A Fledgling Evangelist........................ 59

PART THREE: EARLY MINISTRY 69

Chapter 12: Campus Crusade For Christ 71
Chapter 13: Ministry Begins............................... 83
Chapter 14: Amsterdam '86 And A New Organization 91

BOB MCLAUGHLIN

PART FOUR: MINISTRY EXPANDS **99**

Chapter 15: The Beginning of the End 101
Chapter 16: A Reflection of Jonah In Leningrad 111
Chapter 17: You Are Crocodile Meat 123
Chapter 18: The Bullwhip and National Television News 127
Chapter 19: A Siberian Adventure 135
Chapter 20: You Are An Answer To Prayer 147
Chapter 21: Close Call In Mindanao........................ 153

PART FIVE: TRIALS, ADVERSITIES, & TRIBULATIONS
    TAKE THEIR TOLL **157**

A Preamble To This Section 159
Chapter 22: The Christian Farmer 161
Chapter 23: Our Church Will Pay For It 171
Chapter 24: If You Ever Have A Need....................... 175
Chapter 25: I Will See To It You Never Step Foot In
    This Pulpit Again!................................ 181
Chapter 26: Don't You Think For One Minute That
    You Can Just Come Here To Be Blessed and Fed 187
Chapter 27: Now We Really Have Something
    Very Exciting To Share With You................. 191

PART SIX: THE CRUCIBLE YEARS AND REPENTANCE **197**

Chapter 28: The Storm Approaches......................... 199
Chapter 29: A Secret Sin Exposed......................... 205
Chapter 30: A Painful Separation 211
Chapter 31: Bob, God Is Not Finished With You Yet.......... 217
Chapter 32: A 12-Step Program Begs The Question To The
    Church: Forgiveness – Seventy Times Seven –
    Where Art Thou? 231
Chapter 33: Repentance, Counseling, and A
    Restored Marriage............................. 237

IN THE WAR

**PART SEVEN: ADVERSITY CONTINUES AS HUNDREDS
OF THOUSANDS ARE COMING TO CHRIST** 243

Chapter 34: A Slow Cautious Return 245
Chapter 35: Tensions Arise 257
Chapter 36: The Proposals 261

PART EIGHT: TRIALS AND TRIBULATIONS CONTINUE 267

Chapter 37: Another New Ministry: Salvation
Today Ministries 269
Chapter 38: You Don't Fit The Missionary Profile 275
Chapter 39: He's A Cult-Like Speaker. People Respond
To Him, Not God 281
Chapter 40: What You're Doing Is Dangerous For
Those You Preach To 285
Chapter 41: We Don't Believe Your Numbers 289
Chapter 42: Despite Continued Trials and Tribulations,
We Move Forward Victoriously Into The Battle ... 295
Chapter 43: A Word From Bob's Wife 303

Author's Readers Guide 309
Author's Bio 311

ix

DEDICATION

I dedicate this book to Trudy my faithful loving wife of 49 years and our four children, James, who is now in heaven, Joshua, Priscilla, and Rebekah. I am ever grateful for their undying love for me and encouragement despite my many failures over the years.

Author's Family

About the Book

In The War Wounded but Winning portrays in vivid and brutal honesty the rise and fall and rise again true story of the life of Evangelist Bob McLaughlin.

In this provocative book, Evangelist McLaughlin literately draws the reader into the good, the bad and the ugly of his life.

The authors entire life of failures and victories is a riveting description of human involvement in a spiritual war.

This book will challenge and compel each reader to honestly examine oneself and in doing so they will discover they too are engulphed in an intense spiritual war for their soul, and the souls of all humanity. This war is between good and evil, God and Satan.

Evangelist McLaughlin describes the secret of success in this war is to understand the beautiful truth of "meticulous providence," also known as the "greater good" doctrine.

As a candid conservative evangelist, the author sounds an alarm to each reader whether a believer or nonbeliever, as well as the established church in general.

ENDORSEMENTS

Bob and Trudy "go to them". In doing so, they go where God is at work. Hands are raised all over Africa, not because the people are naïve and easily led or because they are strongly influenced in their community responses or whatever, but because God, in His sovereign wisdom has chosen this time as a great time of harvest in Africa and has sent two of his great reapers to help move souls from being "dead in trespasses and sin" to being "alive in Christ" by the power of the Holy Spirit.

I thank God for Bob and Trudy and count it a privilege to be serving Christ with them. I hope you will prayerfully consider supporting their work.

Yours for the Kingdom,

John Crimmins
International Director
Global Pastor Training
Houston, Texas

Often time in sprints, I watch people wrestle with the degree in which they want to embrace that suffering or not. It's easier to pick the path that doesn't require the difficult thing. I know. I've been there. Without a crystal-clear understanding of why this change is the right thing to do and a deep conviction that it's worth it, it will all just die on the vine.

BOB MCLAUGHLIN

To overcome this, you have to name and unpack your God-centered identity. To know what your unique calling and anointing is. Once you have a firm grip on those answers the path will probably become harder but your convictions to stay on it will be greater. This is what leads to deep and lasting transformation.

This encapsules the thrust of this book about Bob and Trudy McLaughlin and their journey thus far.

Enjoy the read and see the God prints all over their lives and let's examine our God-centered identity as well.

For the Journey!

Gary Janzen,
Executive Director
International Christian Mission Services

Life is a series of choices each with its own set of consequences or rewards and Bob's story highlights this reality well. Honestly sharing about his struggles, mistakes, successes, and frustrations, Bob welcomes the reader in to see for themselves what the Lord can do with those who surrender their lives to His will. Throughout this book the message is clear that the greatest choice we can ever make is the decision to allow Jesus Christ to be Lord of our lives. I recommend this book for anyone who is wanting to see how far the grace of God extends.

Rev. Andy Woodworth
Conference Pastor, Evangelical Mennonite Conference

PREFACE

As I write these words, I must acknowledge that this book has been in the making for many years. Honestly, I never thought I would write it. However, many who know me best have encouraged me to pursue it. Ultimately, I know God is behind this production. I have been told by many that this story will inevitably bring glory to God and will be a help to many struggling souls. So, allow me to tell you something about myself.

My overall purpose in writing this book is to tell my very personal and colorful life story in such a way that it will bring glory to God. In these pages you will read about an exciting life filled with many ups and downs and the consequences of both obedience and disobedience to God. My many failures and victories are recorded in the following pages, but it is a story that I pray will ultimately leave every reader with the hope I have received in the Lord.

Though I did not become a Christian until I was twenty-three years of age, I always sensed, even as a child, that there was a God – one Who was aware of everything about me, including what could or would happen to me. At the time, of course, I had no idea that this was simply childlike faith. I did not know what faith was. Furthermore, I had no inkling that this childlike faith, and the thought that God was aware of everything about me, was related to a theological doctrine of the Judeo-Christian faith. This is a doctrine that is hard for us, as finite humans, to wrap our brains around.

BOB MCLAUGHLIN

The doctrine I am referring to is *the doctrine of meticulous providence*. It is also known as 'the greater good' doctrine. In his book *How God Makes Men,* Patrick Morley explains this doctrine as follows: "From cover to cover, the Bible teaches that nothing happens apart from the will of God. Nothing. That doesn't mean God is necessarily *causing* the thing that's happening to you. He may be, but it's just as likely that someone is using his or her free will to do something evil to you and God is allowing that to happen for a greater good."[1]

The Bible teaches, in Matthew 10:29, that God is aware of even a sparrow when it falls to the ground. Think about that, my friend. You and I are far more important to God than a sparrow – yet God takes note of a seemingly insignificant bird. If this is the case, and I believe it is, how much more important are our lives to God?

Merriam-Webster's Dictionary defines success as "a favorable or desired outcome" of something attempted. The innate desire to succeed is how we human beings are wired.

Our small ministry was rapidly expanding, and my popularity (so I was told) was clearly on the rise.

By the early 1990's world travel had become the norm for my life, and it appeared that the fast track to success was at hand. It was not uncommon for me to have breakfast in Paris, lunch in London and dinner in the upper deck business class of a 747 widebody jetliner while flying over the Atlantic Ocean. This scenario, in the eyes of the world, would unquestionably appear to be the epitome of success.

As an itinerant evangelist I truly sought to fulfill my calling to preach the gospel to as many people as possible in my lifetime. I was willing to go anywhere in the world to preach. Over time, this effort was clearly blessed by God and His favor on our ministry was evident in many ways.

---

[1] Patrick Morley, *How God Makes Men* (Colorado Springs, CO: Multnomah Books, 2013), 26

IN THE WAR

Trudy and I were privileged to be the guests several times on the popular Canadian Christian TV program, *100 Huntley Street,* which aired daily from Toronto, Ontario. Around this same time, Dr. Paul Smith, pastor of the world-renowned The Peoples Church of Toronto, saw us on *100 Huntley Street,* and extended an invitation for me to preach on a Sunday morning at his church. I was more than honored.

As usual, The Peoples Church was packed to capacity that Sunday morning. It was thrilling to know that the service I was about to preach at would be broadcast across the nation and into some of the United States. Upon completion of my message that morning, I extended a public invitation, for those who needed to repent, to do so by coming forward in repentance. Many came in tears and stood at the front. After those, who came forward, were ushered out of the main sanctuary and taken to a room for counseling, Dr. Smith, to my great surprise, took up an impromptu offering for our ministry.

Later that night, while at our hotel, we received a telephone call from Dr. Smith. He informed us that his congregation was obviously in favor of our ministry considering the large offering received that morning. Trudy and I were so surprised at the generous amount – our ministry had never received an offering of that size.

Before he ended the conversation with me that night, he said he would like to ask me a question, to which I replied positively. I could not believe my ears. Dr. Smith extended an invitation to us to conduct an entire month of Sunday morning and evening services at The Peoples Church, to be held later that year in November. I accepted, without hesitation. Following my conversation with him, Trudy and I fell to our knees to thank the Lord for this amazing opportunity. That night we agreed together that our ministry was undoubtedly on the fast track to ultimate success.

November came and the month of services produced a good number of people coming forward, and my popularity was on the

xix

rise. People across the nation watched these services. During that month I was once again invited to appear on *100 Huntley Street*. I accepted and they graciously promoted the remaining services at The Peoples Church.

Then in 1991, The Billy Graham Evangelistic Association (BGEA) invited me to participate in helping to promote Mr. Graham's one-day evangelistic event to be held in Central Park, New York City. Along with several other evangelists, selected by the Graham organization, I preached on the streets of NYC for an entire week, in promotion of the coming event.

Later, Dr. John Wesley White, an associate evangelist with BGEA whom I had met, gave me the opportunity to give my testimony in several of his evangelistic crusades in the United States and Canada.

On the international level, many opportunities began opening to us. This came as such a blessing since opportunities in North America were now diminishing. It was becoming clear to us that things were changing, and sadly, the ministry of evangelists was no longer being used as it had been in past years. Many churches were no longer utilizing the ministry of the gifted evangelist.

From 1990 to 1995 we conducted eighteen evangelistic campaigns throughout the former Soviet Union. God miraculously gave us favor with top evangelical leaders across that country. Over and over God's favor was evidenced. One example of this is from a city in southern Russia where I preached at a one-day crusade which was televised to an estimated viewing audience of over six million people. TV and radio interviews were on the rise.

A year of ministry could average up to seven international campaigns, which meant spending two or three weeks abroad on each trip. I also took numerous domestic trips throughout the United States and Canada. In the eyes of the world, this was clearly a glamorous and exotic lifestyle. Indeed, it was something that many people in the western world strive for and desire.

IN THE WAR

I was an ambassador for God. An ambassador is a person who acts as a representative for a country, a person, a specified activity, etc. But this was not just any activity and the command to become an ambassador for God could not have been clearer. It came to me from the scriptures where I read that I was to *"Go into all the world and preach the gospel to all creation."* (Mark 16:15 NASB) In doing this I wouldn't be representing just an industry, a company or even a country. No, this was a higher calling and assignment. I would be representing Almighty Holy God, and I was to obey His command.

Throughout these pages you will read how the actions of some well-meaning and some not so well-meaning people were used of God to shape us into the people we are today. With regards to those who hurt us in this process, we have been able to forgive them. Admittedly this was difficult, but necessary.

It is my prayer that you will be blessed to see how God can work in one man's life – how He can take a person, who by all appearances was destined to a life of total failure and elevate him to heights of glorious success.

However, that man climbed the pinnacle of success only to fall to the depths of despair, seemingly without any hope. But what is important is that you will read about how God used everything that happened to me for His greater good – how He disciplined me lovingly but firmly and restored me to take His gospel to as many people as possible. I hope that as you read these pages you will come to understand that no matter what happens to you, God has allowed it for reasons known only to Him, and if you will trust Him, I assure you that He will take all that happens to you and use it, not only for His greater good but for your greater good as well.

xxi

INTRODUCTION

Why God chooses to use some of the most unlikely people to accomplish His work on earth is a mystery to us, but who can question Him on these matters? The Bible contains many stories of men and women whom He used in just this way. Our human minds tend to think that they were perhaps not worthy, or not prepared or not the right fit for the job God gave them. But His ways are higher than our ways and this is the true story of one such unlikely individual.

I was born into a poverty-stricken home and then raised in a totally dysfunctional and verbally abusive single-parent family. I developed a serious inferiority complex. I became a chronic alcoholic. I was an immoral, violent, and suicidal small-time criminal. Everything about my life screamed "failure" yet God used me for His glory to preach to tens of thousands of people in Africa, Asia, the Canadian Arctic, Russia, Siberia and other former Soviet countries, and parts of Europe. I am not famous and most likely will remain that way, but God has used me to bring many people to Himself.

The Bible teaches us that the Christian is engaged in an intense spiritual battle. Ephesians 6:12 says, *"For our struggle is not against flesh and blood, but against the rulers, against the powers, against the world forces of this darkness, against the spiritual forces of wickedness in the heavenly places."* (NASB) This book is the story of my struggle in such a spiritual battle. My journey will take you from the sinful years of my childhood and youth to the glory of salvation through Jesus Christ. Sadly, though, the journey then continues through numerous times of trials and tribulations, as well as times of mountain-top joy and valleys of deep despair. As you read through these pages, you will see how at times in my life, I failed miserably and disobeyed God as an act of my own will. These valleys were a direct result of my failure to properly prepare for war by putting on the full armor of God, as instructed in Ephesians 6:11 which says, *"Put on the full armor of God, so that you will be able to stand firm against the schemes of the devil."* (NASB) I failed because, although I was aware that *"...greater is He who is in you than he who is in the world"* (1 John 4:4 NASB), I neglected to tap into this phenomenal power that was available to me, even during my weakest moments. At other times, the devil used crafty tactics (like opposition from within the church, the Body of Christ) to attempt to destroy me.

Yes, for the Christian, this life is a battle. When God raises up His children, whom He intends to use for His glory, Satan, the enemy of God, instructs his army of demons to wage war by fully incorporating all their evil techniques. Satan's aim is to weaken the Christian to keep him from attaining his full potential in Jesus Christ.

The late Harold Ockenga, former Pastor of Park Street Church in Boston, Massachusetts, describes this spiritual war in Faithful in Christ Jesus. (Page 298) "At the believer's conversion he enters as a soldier into what John Bunyan called 'The Holy War.' No soldier has entered a grimmer, more difficult and dangerous war. Salvation as purchased by Christ through His death on the Cross,

with all the attendant, heavenly blessings is ours, yet a terrible spiritual conflict rages between the time of His decisive victory on Calvary over the prince of this world and our final redemption. The conflict is not between the good and bad influences of our nature, or between the good and bad elements in the world, but between the believer and super-human enemies who must be met with supernatural strength."

IN THE WAR

These chapters will show you how God changed my life, only to have the enemy, through his crafty tactics, nearly destroy me, placing me on the shelf of inactivity and despair for many years. However, you will also see how God lovingly, but firmly, disciplined and restored me. It was only by the grace of God, through a miraculous work of His hand, that I was able to return to the Lord and experience restoration.

My journey of restoration was not easy. It took many years of discipline, and my eventual repentance, before God allowed me to return to a ministry, which has sent me and my wife around the globe, with the good news of Christ.

PART ONE
INTO THIS WAR

"Every mistake in war is excusable except for two:
inactivity and a refusal to take a risk.
These two mistakes will cost you the war..."
George Patton

Chapter 1

PLEASE DON'T SHOOT

During the height of the Chechen-Russian war, my Russian team and I set up our headquarters in Vladikavkaz, a city just north of the Georgia border, and only sixty kilometers from Grozny, Chechnya. Vladikavkaz clearly possessed the scars of war. There were many burned out buildings which were once the homes of families. Other buildings were pockmarked, having been riddled with bullets and cannon fire. The war had begun here in this city, when armed Chechen rebels rolled in early one morning and began going systematically from house to house, killing, raping, and ravaging the people of Vladikavkaz.

When we arrived in the city, where some gracious Christians had offered us residence in their home, we were nearing the end of another successful evangelistic campaign. We had conducted evangelistic meetings in several Houses of Culture with hundreds surrendering to Christ, including many Russian soldiers. It was almost overwhelming to see these uniformed young men walk the aisle with their heads bowed and their military hats in their hands. Several had tears streaming down their faces as they repented and gave their hearts to Christ. I remember thinking that many of those men wouldn't survive the war.

On our last full day of ministry, I was excited to travel to a small remote village located on the Russian-Chechen border, where we planned to conduct evangelistic meetings. We loaded up our equipment into three Russian Lada vehicles. I rode in the lead vehicle with my interpreter and a Russian Baptist pastor. The rest of our team members occupied the other two vehicles. We travelled on a rough dirt road, skirting the Russian-Chechen border, for an hour or so. As we neared the village where we were to minister, we suddenly and unexpectedly came upon a military blockade in the road. The Russian soldier in charge approached our vehicle and informed us, in pretty good broken English, that we should not enter the village. He was very courteous and told us he knew who we were and that he was pleased that we were ministering to his people. However, he insisted adamantly, but not rudely, that we turn around and go back to the city for the sake of our own safety. When I questioned him as to why we shouldn't go into the village, he pointed to the hills just off in the distance and on our right and said, "Do you see those hills? Sniper fire has been raining into the village from those hills all day. We have orders to encourage you to not enter the village. And besides," he continued, "all the people in the village have taken refuge, barricading themselves in their homes. No one has ventured outside all day."

I felt we had to ask a very important question. "Sir, are you ordering us to stay out of the village?"

His reply surprised us. "No, you are free to decide, but we strongly recommend that you go back to the city."

We discussed the situation as a team and one pastor asked me if I was afraid to go in? I replied, "No," and returned the same question to all of them. The answer was a firm 'no,' without any hesitation. We decided to go in, believing that God had called us to preach the gospel to the people of this village. After all, they were expecting us, the advance preparations had been made, and we had already secured the House of Culture for our meeting.

Reluctantly, the soldiers opened the blockade and we proceeded slowly into the village. It was like a ghost town. There was

IN THE WAR

not a single person to be seen; nor did anyone come to greet us. With our eyes glancing towards the hills, we got out of our vehicles and began to unload our equipment. As we approached the doors of the House of Culture, we realized that we were faced with the possibility that no one would come to the meeting. Who could blame them? The people would have to walk through the open square to enter the House of Culture. We began to develop a plan. We decided to leave the doors to the hall wide open and to open all the windows, so the people could hear the music and the message. However, we realized that even if we did all that, the sound would be muffled. One of the pastors suggested that we put the speakers outside, but we realized that the villagers would then be able to hear us, yet still could not see us. So, we all decided, why not just set up in the village square and conduct the meeting out in the open? Though this decision carried great risks, it was truly of the Lord.

We set up the speakers facing the hills and made an announcement to the snipers. We told them that we had come to tell everyone, including them, how much God loves them. We said, "Please don't shoot! Please put your weapons down and listen to the music and this life-changing message of God's love for you."

One of the pastors opened the meeting in prayer, after which the Russian music group, who came with us, began singing. Their beautiful harmonies flooded the village and rose up into the hills. Slowly we could see curtains being pulled back, and the windows opening a little more with each song. Then to our great surprise, the doors of the houses began to open and one by one the people of the village began to walk outside and into the village square. By the time I stood to preach the gospel, the entire village stood before me. Several hundred men, women and children boldly and fearlessly stood in the open square and clearly in the sights of the snipers, to listen to God's message of love and salvation.

After giving a simple gospel message, I was holding back tears as I extended the invitation to the people to repent and come

5

forward to receive Christ. The entire village, many with tears in their eyes, came forward and reverently bowed their heads as I encouraged them to surrender their lives to Christ. I then turned to face the hills where the snipers were and said, "Thank you for not shooting. This message is for you too. You can also repent and receive Christ right where you are. God loves you all." I told them that I was going to lead them in a simple prayer of repentance and that they could repeat the prayer and receive Christ. After I prayed, I let them know that if they had prayed that prayer, then they now belonged to the family of God and were our brothers and sisters in Christ.

On this side of heaven, we may never know how many snipers or villagers gave their hearts to Christ that day, but my God does. All glory, honor, and praise to Him.

Preaching in Russia

Chapter 2

GET ON THE FLOOR AND LICK THAT UP LIKE A DOG

I was born on June 22, 1951, in Plymouth, New Hampshire. At the time, my family was staying at my grandmother's little summer cottage on Route 175, a secondary road connecting the towns of Plymouth and Holderness. I was told that my father had been drinking all that day and had left the house with friends to continue drinking somewhere else. So when it came time for my arrival, a neighbor offered to take my mom to the hospital. Mom told me that I was a sickly baby and nearly died from pneumonia, so I spent several weeks in the hospital. Shortly after my release from the hospital we moved back to Boston.

I spent the first few years of my life frequently moving back and forth from Boston to Quincy, Massachusetts, and eventually to Holderness, NH. As I understand it, my father was constantly in and out of trouble with the law and could not hold a job. This, of course, contributed to our frequent moving, thus creating painful instability.

The year was 1955, and we were now living in South Boston, or 'Southey', as it was affectionately referred to. Our apartment was small and sparsely furnished. One day, I remember my mom preparing supper – a simple spaghetti meal. My brother John and

I were cheerfully playing together when our father came home. The happy time we were enjoying quickly dissipated as his very presence brought with it an unwanted atmosphere of uneasiness, bordering on fear. At the time, I was too young to fully understand why he caused these feelings in our home. It would not be until later, that I would learn most of the reasons for his behavior.

My father was an alcoholic and addicted to drugs. He was a criminal, of sorts, with a short fuse and a fiery Irish temper that could flare up at the drop of a hat, especially when he had been drinking. My father and his brothers were involved in the Boston crime scene. In fact, when I was older, my mom showed me a copy of a Boston newspaper with a picture of the police holding two men at gun point with their hands up. The men were my father's brothers, who had been caught while attempting to commit a robbery in Boston. I have since learned that the McLaughlin brothers were very well known to the city police as well as the state police. There were also rumors that they ran with the Boston Irish gangs. At the age of sixty-four, my father died while serving time in prison, and was buried in a pauper's grave in Boston.

When we sat down for supper that evening, my father took the seat at one end of the table; mom was on my right and my brother John was on my left. What happened next has been forever etched in my mind and I will never forget it. I was a typical little boy who loved to be creative and adventurous. Eating spaghetti was a lot of fun for me. I began lifting the noodles on my fork and watched with interest as each noodle slid off a prong. I added to the fun by building a small pile of noodles on the floor, thinking that it was going unnoticed by my family.

Suddenly, I startled as I heard my father slam his fist on the table. He barked at me, "Get down on the floor and lick up that spaghetti like a dog, NOW!" Trembling with fear, I jumped down and began to do as my father had commanded.

IN THE WAR

At that point, my mom exclaimed, "Joseph, I will not allow our son to lick food off the floor like a dog!"

That is when it happened! My father kicked back his chair as he stood, and with one swift sweep of his arm, he cleared most of the table of its glasses, silverware, dishes, drink, and food. Everything went crashing to the floor. Mom blurted out to my brother, "Take Robby and run to the bedroom!" John scooped me up in his arms and carried me to the bedroom where we hid under a dresser. He held me in his arms and assured me that it was going to be all right. I remember how frightened I was and how we trembled in each other's arms as we listened to the horrible sounds coming from the kitchen. The sickening sound of my father's fists hitting my dear mom, her screams, and his cursing were almost too frightening to bear. Then the noise continued with the crashing of more dishes as well as pots and pans. Soon the door slammed, and my father was gone. The kitchen, which was the scene of the horrific argument, would have been in a terrible mess and maybe even had spatters of blood. Thankfully though, by God's mercy, I do not remember the rest of that terrible evening. However, I do remember one thing – there was a peace that accompanied the fact that he was gone.

Later that year, sometime after the birth of my little sister Elizabeth, mom moved our family back to New Hampshire. We were very poor, so we were forced to live in absolute poverty in a two-room shack. It had been vacant for many months, and I remember the musty smell when we opened the door and walked in. Mom did the best she could to make it feel like a home. The little shack had no running water or indoor plumbing. There was an outhouse a short distance away and water was carried from a neighboring well. We burned wood in the kitchen stove and in a small potbelly stove in the second room, which doubled as the living room and our bedroom. 'Nana,' my dear grandmother who was living with us, slept on a cot in the kitchen.

Times were hard, but it just seemed normal to me. I really did not fully realize just how poverty-stricken we were. Mom endured many hardships while raising her children, but she did the best she could with what she had. As an adult, I look back and respect her so much for the many sacrifices she made for us kids.

I remember that every now and then we would walk the two miles to the town of Plymouth to do some shopping. Mom would place my little sister in a wagon and off we'd go. She liked to make a game out of the journey. So, as we walked along, we were to look for as many soda pop and beer bottles as we could find, and place them in the wagon. This was a lot of fun for me, but I did not know that the number of groceries we purchased that week, often depended on the number of bottles we found. Mom traded in the bottles for a small cash refund, which allowed her to purchase a few more items of groceries.

Once we finished the shopping, we would begin our long walk back home. Sometimes we stopped to buy milk at a small dairy farm. I really liked going into the farmhouse; it had this incredible typical farmhouse smell. I would run over to the big tub which held the bottles of milk, submerged in ice cold water. Mr. Huckins, the dairy farmer, would lift me up so I could lean over the edge of the tub, and reach into the cold water to pull out one or two bottles of milk. I was always so excited to get home with the milk because we could drink the cream off the top of each bottle. And maybe, if my mom was able to buy some, we could have cookies too.

I have daily memories of seeing mom carrying buckets of water, one in each hand, to the house. In the winter it was not uncommon to see her splitting and bringing in the wood. Every morning mom would take two buckets out to the outhouse. The one kept under the cast iron sink was what she called the 'slop bucket.' The other – well, it was called the 'honey bucket.' Despite its name, it was the bucket that smelled the worst, since it had been 'used' the whole previous day and night. I hated that bucket the most.

I can remember watching, wide-eyed, as mom and nana killed chickens. Nana held the chicken down and stretched its neck across a tree stump while mom swung the axe, and zip – off came its head. Oh, how I grimaced every time the axe came down. Soon however, I was jumping with glee as I watched the poor chicken run and even try to fly! It was my job to catch the headless creature.

One summer, my mom encouraged my brother John to start a small business to help provide some income. However, she made it mandatory that we all join in on the work. Every few days or so, we would all go down into the nearby woods to dig worms. John would put a sign out by the road – "Worms for Sale – 1 cent each." I hated the worm digging business, but I had to pick up the slimy cold worms and deposit them into a coffee can. Picking up worms was not the reason I hated the job – it was the wretched mosquitoes – they used to eat us alive!

As I got older, I began doing most of the chores, and eventually, all the chores became my responsibility; I hated them with a passion.

My father was not in the picture after we moved to New Hampshire, but one day, when I was 6 years old, he came to visit for a weekend. He ended up drunk and passed out behind the shed. The police came to arrest him and took him away; I never saw him again.

Unknown to me, these days of being raised in a single-parent home were truly days of simply surviving, for our family. Yet, I didn't really have any serious problems that I knew of. That is, not until I began school in the fall of 1957.

Chapter 3

HE'S JUST LIKE HIS FATHER

I really did love my mother and over the years I developed a deep respect for her. It was only as I entered my adult years that I learned about all she went through as a child growing up in Boston. She was one of eight children and her father, my grandfather, George Brooks, was an alcoholic; that resulted in instability and the inability to provide proper care for his large family. This neglect eventually became known to the authorities in the State of Massachusetts. Consequently, the State stepped in and removed the younger children, placing them in foster homes. This was a painful and traumatic time for all of the family members. Witnessing the removal of her little brothers and sisters and the breakup of her entire family deeply affected my mom. Although she was a young girl herself, she was determined to do all she could to help her mom get the children back from the State. Consequently, and against her mother's wishes, she decided to quit school in grade eight. She took on as many odd jobs as she could secure, working day and night for the next full year. The hard work of my mom and grandmother together enabled them to raise the quality of living in their home. They eventually met the State's required standards suitable for a family, and the children were returned home. Unfortunately, for my mom, she never went back to school and simply continued to help support the family.

After some time, she met and fell in love with a young man. Sadly, before long she discovered that she was pregnant. Who the father of that child (my brother John) was, has always been a mystery to me? As I recall, he was never talked about, and I have no information about him. I do remember that, as a teenager, I did ask my mom, "Whatever happened to John's dad?"

Her response was, "Oh, he was killed in the war." Apparently, she told me a lie, maybe because she thought I was too young to understand the truth. I believed her answer until the day she finally told me and my sister the truth. We learned that John was an illegitimate child, and that when his father (we were never told his name) found out about the pregnancy, he insisted that Mom have the baby aborted. She refused and would not even consider it, so he promptly left her to fend for herself. She later gave birth to her first child and named him John Brooks, using her maiden's name, since the father was not around.

After the end of WWII, my mom met and married a war veteran, Wendell Davis, and they had a son, Larry. Wendell was a typical casualty of WWII. Though he survived the war physically, he was haunted by memories of the atrocities he experienced. He most likely suffered from what is now commonly known as PTSD (post-traumatic stress disorder). Like so many returning war vets, he would 'self-medicate' with alcohol. Sadly, when not at work, alcohol became his constant friend as he attempted to ease his conscience of the horrifying memories. Unfortunately, this soon led to a separation and later, divorce.

Even though Wendell had a serious drinking problem and exhibited some violent outbursts, he somehow convinced the state that his son, Larry, would be better off in his custody. On Larry's first birthday, while mom was having a little party for him, the police

IN THE WAR

came and officially took Larry away, placing him in the custody of his father. I can only imagine the pain my mom suffered as a result.

At the time that we were moving back to New Hampshire – a few weeks after the spaghetti supper fight when my father, Joseph, walked out of the door – Mom felt it was necessary to inform me that I had another brother, besides John. She told me his name was Larry and that he lived in New Hampshire with his father, Wendell Davis. When I heard this, I had only one question – would I get to meet Larry as soon as we got to New Hampshire. Mom assured me that I would see him because he was going to be our neighbor. Wow, I had another brother!

On weekends I would visit Larry, but I remember that Wendy (that is what we all called his dad) would almost always be drunk. It was when he was drinking that he would cry and talk of buddies who were killed in the war. Wendy, like so many who survived the horrors of war, had to deal with deep feelings of guilt, never really understanding why they were the ones who came home alive.

Personally, I really liked Wendy – he was always kind to me. I also greatly appreciated his generosity at Christmas time. From the time I turned thirteen years of age, until I moved out of my mom's home, he always gave me two packs of Lucky Strike cigarettes for Christmas. Yes, my mom had given me permission to smoke when I turned twelve years old. She told me that she knew I had been smoking for a long time, (I had my first smoke when I was six) so I might as well smoke in her presence.

So, this was our family – my two brothers: John Brooks and Larry Davis; and the three of us who were fathered by Joseph McLaughlin: me, another son who died at birth and my sister Elizabeth. Clearly, this was a very dysfunctional family consisting of four living children, three different fathers and only one mother.

When I look back to those days, I realize that my mom was a young woman who had struck out three times, so to speak, and yet she had grit. She was determined to raise her children in the best circumstances possible. Many young women in her situation would have abandoned us kids and sought after the pleasures of life that are offered to them. I truly thank God for my mom, even with all the mistakes she made.

Once I reached school age, it didn't take me long to sense that I was different than the rest of my siblings. My little sister naturally got a lot of attention since she was the baby. My big brother John was six years older than me and appeared to receive more attention than I did. At least that is how I perceived it. There seemed to be something about me that made me feel like I just did not fit in. I can only assume it was classic middle child syndrome. No matter what John did, it was fine, whereas I, on the other hand, could not seem to do much of anything that was pleasing to my mom. I can still hear her saying, "He's just like his father!" or "Look at that – that's his father all over again, isn't it?" Even my brother John would often make similar statements. It didn't matter who they were talking to, they would just go ahead and blurt out these negative comments anyways.

There really isn't anything wrong with pointing out certain behavioral traits of a child which tend to be characteristic of his or her parents. When it is done in a positive manner, pointing out a good trait can be extremely beneficial to the development of the child's character. Affirming and building up a child is healthy for them. Unfortunately, these remarks were meant in a negative sense. So, every time I did something 'bad,' I could always count on John or my mom to say, "He's just like his father."

At that time, I had no idea of what was happening to me because of constantly hearing this criticism. To fully understand how it affected me in a negative way throughout my childhood, you must understand the following. Whenever my father's name was brought up in conversation in our home, the remarks were never positive, but always negative. Not once did I ever hear a positive comment about him. His name was almost like a swear word in our home. So,

IN THE WAR

it's not difficult to see how growing up in this kind of an environment could influence a young boy negatively, and it did.

I wished I could locate my father so I could hear his side of the story, but this was something I would never be able to do. So, the years went by and I constantly heard that I was like this awful man who was my father. I really believe my mom and John were unaware of the damage they inflicted on me at that time. And, I had no idea of the long-term negative influence this would have on my future. Even though I swore that I would never be like my father, the inevitable happened and I was becoming "just like my father."

Chapter 4

WHEN DO I GO HOME?

I was excited and a little frightened when my first day of school arrived. There was no preschool or kindergarten in our area of New Hampshire, so I entered grade one in early September of 1957.

The Holderness Central School was just a couple of miles up Route 175 as we headed towards the town of Holderness. My brothers had told me all about school and I was ready to experience it firsthand, or so I thought. Unfortunately, I got off to a bad start and here is how I remember it.

I recall being a bit overwhelmed with meeting so many new children and adults all in one day. This was a totally foreign environment for me. I made it through the day but was happy when it was time to go home. I remember that, after the bell rang, we all lined up to get on the bus. I boarded the bus with my big brother John, and we selected seats near the back. After the bus started to move, I decided to stand up and look around. Apparently, this was an infraction of the rules and caught the attention of the bus monitor, who shouted at me to sit down! I was not used to anyone outside my own family telling me what to do, so without any hesitation, I shouted back to her, "Leave me alone!" I also called her a bad name. Well, that was a huge mistake! I shouted so loudly that the entire bus heard me, including Mr. Hunt, the bus driver, who immediately stopped the bus.

John just looked at me with total disbelief, not to mention shock, and said, "Oh boy, Robby, you've really done it now!"

Mr. Hunt was a big man – not fat, but tall with broad shoulders. When he stood up at the front of the bus that day, my heart began to pound. I knew I was in big trouble. I sank down into my seat as Mr. Hunt began to give a lecture regarding school bus behavior. He explained that he did not tolerate the kind of language he had just heard, and that we were to respectfully obey the school bus monitors. I was relieved that he did not come down to my seat and make an example out of me.

I learned that Mr. Hunt really was a genuinely nice man, and we got along fine in the years following that incident. As it turned out, when I was in the eighth grade, he gave me the job of bus monitor. Then, when I graduated from elementary school, he gave me $5.00, and in 1966 that was a whole lot of money

Education was something I would not learn to appreciate until much later in life. My mom had dropped out of school in grade eight, so consequently she wasn't able to provide the help I needed with my studies. My brother John also quit school early. In the tenth grade, he went to work in the local sawmill to help support the family, so he was also unable to help me. As a result, I was basically left on my own to get through school and I didn't get off to a good start. I failed grade one and had to repeat it the following year. I always resented the fact that I was the only one out of my class who was held back. It was difficult for me, because I really felt sad that my class went on without me.

I hated school and certainly did not apply myself as I should have, so school was difficult for me. As far back as I can remember, the moment I sat down at my desk, one thought often ran through my mind: *When do I go home?*

IN THE WAR

In elementary school I began to develop an inferiority complex. I wore hand-me-down clothes from my brother John, while all the other kids had brand new clothes, so I became envious and felt inferior to them. I envied these kids because of their clothes, their nice homes with running water and indoor plumbing, and because they belonged to functional families, with a mom and a dad.

I remember the first time I saw the twins' home. (The 'twins' were Mr. Hunt's daughters.) We were out on a class trip, and while on our way back to the school, he stopped the bus beside his house to let the twins off. I just sat there, looking out the window at that beautiful home. It looked more like a resort to me, since the Hunts owned a beautiful motel with a swimming pool. We all waved goodbye to the girls as they stood on the driveway in front of their beautiful white house, located beside the motel and that gorgeous swimming pool, with its blue water dancing and sparkling in the sunshine. Envy washed over me, and I wished with all my heart that my home was like theirs.

I managed to make it through the nine years of elementary schooling, but in all those years, I never invited any of my class-mates to come to my house to play, because I would have been totally embarrassed. I just could not bear the thought of someone coming to my place, and that during their visit they would need to use our terrible smelling outhouse!

Looking back, I can clearly understand how much I hated the environment I was forced to live in. Yet ironically, nearly every day while in school, I would sit and stare at the big clock on the wall with that question on my mind: *When do I go home?*

Chapter 5

I HATE THIS LIFE!

"I hate this life!" I remember the first time that I said those words and really meant them. It was a very stormy winter day. I was about eleven years old – happy to have finished my school day and to arrive at home. As I walked through the door, and before I could remove my coat and boots, I heard my mom say, "Robby, we need water." These were not the first words that I wanted to hear on my return from school. I threw my books down and grabbed the two large pails that I used every day to carry water. The storm had produced a good amount of heavy wet snow, so I was dreading the task before me, as I went out the door.

    I trudged through the deep snow – down the hill, between our neighbor's sheds and up the path to the well. When I got there, the first thing I had to do was shovel all the snow off the top of the well. Once this was done, I lifted the heavy trap door and leaned it against the brace, which had been built behind the opening, to hold the door in place. Next, I took the twelve-foot pole, with a bucket attached to the end, and lowered it into the well, hand over hand. Once the bucket was full, I pulled it up, hand over hand, and filled the empty pails. I then closed the well's cover and began the trek back to the house with a full pail of water in each hand. When I was past the sheds, I began to struggle up the hill to our little two-room shack. Halfway up, my arms began to weaken so that I could no longer keep the full pails from dragging in the snow. As a result, the snow started to build up on the bottom and edges of the pails, and they began tipping and spilling water into my boots. I could not contain my anger any longer. At this point I set the pails down, grabbed them one at a time and threw them as far as I could. I looked up at the sky and screamed, "I hate this life!"

I was shouting at God, and I knew it. I told Him how unfair I thought He was. I asked Him why He had placed me in such a messed-up family, and why we lived in a two-room shack with all these despicable chores. I continued shouting and swearing, but there was no response. Reluctantly, I retrieved the pails, made the trip back to the well, got the water again and returned to the house. I was angry!

The words, "I hate this life!" would become a frequent cry throughout my childhood. I developed an intense hatred towards my father. I hated school. I hated the shack and junkyard I was forced to live in. I hated the fact that there was no privacy in a cramped, two-room shack, where Sunday night baths were in a round, tin tub in the middle of the kitchen floor, beside the wood stove. I hated the other kids in my school for having a better life than I had. I hated knowing that everyone thought I was just like my father.

Hating my life wasn't helped by the strained relationship I had with my brother John. He had quit school in the tenth grade and was now working long hours in the local sawmill. He strongly felt that he needed to go to work, so he could help support mom and us kids. His new role as a provider for the family dramatically affected our relationship as brothers, and it didn't take me long to notice this significant change. It was obvious to me, that once he began working, he assumed it was also his responsibility to become more of a father figure in the home. So, the result is, I lost a brother and gained a father figure I did not want. This unwelcome

IN THE WAR

and unexpected change generated a very rebellious attitude in my heart. Consequently, our brotherly love began fading rapidly, resulting in very intense arguments at times and ongoing conflicts over the years. Clearly there was a wedge between us, and sadly, it festered with the passing of time, causing a bitter separation to continue for many years to come.

I just hated life! In fact, I hated my life so much that I remember praying at night, asking God to allow me to simply die in my sleep, so I could escape this miserable life. Only later did I realize just how much God was listening to my cry for help.

Broken promises were another disturbing reality of my young life. I totally despised being misled or misinformed, but I'm not sure why these things happened. I can only speculate that perhaps Mom and John had so much pain from their experience with my father, that they took their frustrations out on me, simply because, in their eyes, I was so much like him.

Two broken promises stand out in my mind. The first one was on my twelfth birthday, which ended up being an extremely sad day for me. I was told that I would get a brand-new bike for my birthday, and I was really looking forward to that day. June 22, 1963, came and went as I waited all day for that new bike. As the day wore on, hope began to fade. I did have a cake with candles, but the bike never showed up. No one ever mentioned the promised bike again, and I never questioned why. I went to bed that night – an angry boy, who hurt all over.

Day after day, I found myself struggling with deep feelings of hurt and disappointment: *Maybe my mom really wanted to get me a new bike, but just could not afford it,* I would reason. *Or perhaps she was just too proud to admit that she couldn't afford a bike.* She never gave me an explanation, and eventually I began to believe they were teasing me out of spite.

Another promise my mom broke was even more devastating to me. Christmas of 1965 was the worst Christmas of my young

25

BOB MCLAUGHLIN

life. During the previous summer, I had earned a few dollars doing small, odd jobs around the neighborhood. I managed to save about $20.00 and purchased a small, cheap, six-string acoustic guitar for $17.50. Because I possessed a natural talent for music and art, I was able to quickly learn how to play the guitar, strictly by ear. It was not long before I wanted to own an electric guitar. I'd mention that I would really like to have one someday, to which Mom and John would reply, "Well, Christmas is just around the corner." This was their response time and time again. I should have known better, but I started hoping, and eventually believing, that maybe they were planning to purchase an electric guitar as a Christmas gift for me. I guess I wanted to believe that no one would deliberately lie and give false hope to a young boy.

Christmas Eve arrived, and I could hardly contain my excitement. I vividly remember watching that evening, as my mom and brother brought gifts over to our place, from nana's cottage next door, and placed them under the tree. As they came into the house they would laugh and say, "Hey, look out, don't damage that new electric guitar." They really made a big deal out of it and sadly, I swallowed it hook, line and sinker.

I was so happy when I went to bed that Christmas Eve that I could hardly contain myself. I awoke with so much excitement on Christmas morning, only to go to bed that night, broken-hearted. I remember John and mom just grinning at me every time I looked at them during the day. I soon discovered there was no electric guitar at all, and nothing was ever said about it again. I pushed the anger and hurt way down inside of me and refused to show it to them. The rest of that day was miserable, but I never let on that I was so deeply hurt. However, I never forgot it, and I never understood how anyone could deliberately hurt a family member the way they hurt me. I was beginning to hate this life more and more!

26

IN THE WAR

My mom with our children

Chapter 6

SEARCHING FOR ACCEPTANCE

All of humanity has an innate need to be loved, accepted, and appreciated for who they are as a person. These needs do not dissipate once we mature into adulthood; they are with us for our entire life. We may tend to express them differently, but the bottom line is, we still have the same basic needs.

Like most kids, I craved attention as I struggled along in my young life. I needed to understand where I fit into this thing called 'life.' I hungered for love, appreciation, and acceptance, but from what I have already written about some of my childhood, you can see that it was rather difficult to find this desperately needed love and acceptance at home with my family.

Although I hated school, that is where I found a measure of what I craved. One day, our first-grade teacher asked us to draw a picture. We could draw anything we wanted. I picked up my pencil and started to draw, just as the teacher had instructed. When I finished, I raised my hand, so the teacher came over, stood by my desk and with a big smile she said, "My, my, my, Robert, you are a very talented little artist!" I was not exactly sure what an artist was, but I really liked how she reacted to my picture. I was even more surprised at my mom's response to the same drawing when I brought it home a few days later. She really thought it was beautiful and encouraged me to continue drawing. I was quite proud of my accomplishment.

It did not take long for my classmates to see that I had a special, natural talent. Soon I was receiving the attention I craved. The other kids would often say, "I wish I could draw like you." I liked hearing them say this; I could do something better than they could! But strangely, I felt sorry for them.

I was not an exceptionally good academic student. In fact, the only A's I received on my report cards were for penmanship and art. I was a terrible speller, but my writing was superb. I was always glad to see the penmanship teacher arrive once a month. He would walk down the aisle and grade the papers, which were waiting for him on our desks. I loved watching him write a big, bright red A+ on my paper, right beside the C-, D or even an F, that I got as the grade for the paper's content.

Another natural talent emerged during the fifth grade. An elderly, white-haired man, by the name of Mr. Bush, came to our school to look for students who were interested in learning to play a musical instrument. I was astounded at his ability to play so many different instruments, but it was when he played the violin that I really sat up and took notice. I just loved the sound he could produce, and I immediately signed up to take violin lessons. As soon as I held the instrument in my hand, I knew that I would do well at playing it. Mr. Bush agreed and said, "You have a very natural talent for music, young man!" From that moment on, I was determined to master the violin.

My mom also supported me in this venture, even to the point of purchasing a $70.00 brand new violin for me. I am not sure, but I think Mr. Bush may have helped to pay for it. In fact, he may have paid the entire bill. It was not long before I was playing solos on the gym stage during school programs. I literally ate up the applause of the audience. There was something magical about entertaining and receiving the positive response.

IN THE WAR

By the time I entered high school in the fall of 1966, I was also playing guitar. My love for rock and roll music led me to join a local band, where I sang back-up vocals and played both the electric violin and rhythm guitar. I became popular and the sound of applause appealed to my fleshly desires. Our band was well known since we played at many of the weekend dance canteens, as well as the college and university frat parties. We even won a few Battles of the Bands – a statewide contest for bands where the youth voted for the one they thought was the best. We also appeared on *New Hampshire Bandstand*, a weekly television program. The popular show was a takeoff of Dick Clark's famous *American Bandstand* and consisted of youth dancing to the sounds of rock and roll music played by the local state band, that was featured that day.

In 1967, a twenty-minute folk-rock song by Arlo Guthrie, entitled "Alice's Restaurant," came out. I memorized the entire song and performed it, as a solo with my guitar, in front of over five hundred high school students and faculty during a Friday afternoon assembly. I will never forget the thunderous applause and the standing ovation I received in the gym that afternoon. It was a game changer for me. I thought I had finally found the way to acceptance and popularity – the spotlight of performing on stage! However, after a couple of years, two of our band members left for university, causing our popular band to break up. My newfound popularity took a steep nosedive, leaving me feeling like a failure again. As my world collapsed, I increased my dabbling in glue and gasoline sniffing as well as my marijuana and alcohol use, and once again, I was back to searching for acceptance.

PART TWO
CONVERSION

Chapter 7

TWO MEN PRAYED AND GOD ANSWERED

John, a soft-spoken, humble man, was a Baptist lay minister at a country church in central New Hampshire. He was also a faithful member of Gideons International, a Christian association. He was employed by a small power company where his day-to-day activities involved reading power meters and recording their power usage. Each meter had to be read once a month for billing purposes.

One day, while reading the meter attached to a small, dilapidated, two-room shack, he could sense that someone was watching him. He was relieved when he saw that it was a small boy, five or six years of age, who was staring at him. The little boy was clearly a picture of poverty. His hair was dirty and matted, his face was grimy and tear-stained, and his clothing was tattered and torn. At the sight of the young lad, John's tender, Christian heart broke for him and his poverty-stricken, single-parent family who lived in the shack.

John smiled and said, "Hi, little fellow," which caused the boy to run away and hide out of sight. His quick response to the greeting brought on an even broader smile to John's face. He finished writing down the information that he needed from the meter, but then, before he could return to his truck to leave, the Holy Spirit spoke clearly and firmly to John's heart. He said, "I want you to pray for that little boy. I have plans for him. I'm going to use him in a powerful way." John immediately bowed his head and prayed, just as God had told him to do. Since his job required that the meter be read monthly, it provided a perfect reminder to pray for the little boy and his entire family as instructed by the Holy Spirit. So John faithfully obeyed the Holy Spirit's prompting that day, and made it a point to pray for the family every month. His special prayers continued month after month and year after year.

Fast forward twelve years to a hot and humid July night in the summer of 1969. That same little boy was now one of several highly intoxicated teenagers staggering down the main street of a small New England town. Cursing and swearing, these small-town thugs were itching for a confrontation with anyone who would have the misfortune of meeting them on the street. They all had earned a bad reputation as troublemakers and were known to the residents and the police. People would often cross the street rather than endure the pure harassment of these local hooligans. That night, they staggered through the doors of the local pizza restaurant. Once inside, they couldn't resist making derogatory remarks to the poor girl behind the counter, while she took their order. The restaurant began to clear out quickly as these obnoxious, foul-mouthed teens also began to taunt the other customers.

Soon, one of the fellows, who had earlier consumed a tremendous amount of alcohol, passed out, slid off his chair to the floor and vomited all over himself. This proved to be the last straw. The manager shouted, "I'm calling the police! Get your drunken friend out of here – NOW!" Surprised by his outburst, they dragged their unconscious friend out to the sidewalk and wondered what to do with him before the police arrived. One of them suggested that they take him across the street to the old Inn. This seemed to be the best solution to their problem. So, they dragged him to the Inn and up the wooden steps to the porch. When they opened the door, they noticed that, even though the lights were on in the foyer, no one was visible. They quickly hauled their friend in and deposited him on a couch in the reception area, and then they vacated the premises.

Upon hearing the commotion, the manager of the Inn came out of his office only to find an intoxicated and clearly unconscious teenager stretched out on the couch, with vomit all over himself. Mr. Calvin walked across the reception area, shaking his head. He looked down at the teen and immediately recognized him. He knew of the young man's reputation and was now faced with a major decision to make: should he call the authorities and have him placed in jail for the night, or should he call on the ultimate authority – Holy God? You see, Mr. Calvin was a lay Pentecostal preacher; he decided to call on the Lord. He humbly knelt beside the couch and laid his hands on the foul-smelling teenager and prayed, as only a Pentecostal preacher can pray. He asked the Lord to save the young man's soul, anoint him with God's power, and send him around the world as a preacher of the Gospel.

When he finished praying, he knew God's love was compelling him to take pity on the teen. He carried the young man up the stairs to an empty room and placed him on the bed. He took a wet cloth and cleaned the vomit from his face and clothing. He covered him with a clean blanket and positioned his head on the pillow so that, if he were to vomit, he would not choke on it. He kept vigil all night in prayer, and every half hour or so he would climb the stairs to check on him.

Early the next morning, the young man woke up, hungover, confused, and unable to recall the events of the night before. Eventually, he realized where he was but could not recall how he got there. He quickly vacated the Inn through the back door and made his way home.

Years passed and this same young man now had a totally different life. He and his wife had become Christians and had discovered an intimate relationship with Jesus. They had two children and the young man, whose name is Bob, had secured a job at a power company. Yes, the little boy and the drunken teenager were none other than me.

Some will undoubtedly wonder how I came to know about the two men who prayed for me. After all, I was only a small child when John began praying for me, and I was drunk and passed out when Mr. Calvin prayed over me.

As I mentioned earlier, John worked for a power company, and I was able to secure a job with that company shortly after becoming a Christian. He no longer read meters but was now working in the company office. As it happened, John and I not only worked for the same company, but we worked in the same office. After a few days at my new job, he approached me saying he wanted to share an exciting, true story with me. We agreed to meet during coffee break in the lunchroom. John told me of his encounter with the Holy Spirit, at my childhood home, many years before. He said how happy he was that, after all these years, God had answered his persistent prayers. I thanked him with a heart full of gratitude and we rejoiced together. I was amazed at how God had moved a concerned and obedient Christian to pray for me all those years.

A couple of months later, I was invited to attend a men's prayer breakfast for a special event that was coming to our community. It turned out that Mr. Calvin attended the same meeting. Once he realized who I was, he approached me and said, "Do I have a story for you!" Once again, I sat there, amazed and with my heart full of overwhelming joy, as I listened to yet another true story of how God had worked in my life. Mr. Calvin unfolded the events of that night, which had occurred a few years before – a night that I couldn't even remember. I had always wondered how I ended up in that room in the Inn on that shameful night. I knew that I had been left on the couch in the reception area, because my friends told me about it a few days later but waking up in a bed on the second floor is

IN THE WAR

what baffled me. With tears of appreciation welling up in my eyes, I thanked Mr. Calvin for obeying God on my behalf.

So, friend, don't ever underestimate the power of prayer. The Bible is filled with stories of answered prayer. You can know that when you pray to our heavenly Father, He hears and answers. And when God prompts you to pray fervently for someone or something – do it! Yes, He may answer quickly, or He may answer much later than you want, but He will answer at the perfect time – HIS time.

"This is the confidence which we have before Him, that if we ask anything according to His will, He hears us. And if we know that He hears us in whatever we ask, we know that we have the requests which we have asked from Him." (1 John 5:14 & 15 NASB)

Chapter 8

A NEW BEGINNING

Looking back on my life, I can see how it really began to spiral out of control when I was a young man. I had entered a life of petty crime at a very young age, then later dropped out of high school and joined a small-town gang of hooligans. My world escalated into a wretched state of alcohol, drugs, immoral living, violence, jail time and a lengthy police record which I had accumulated. I attempted to get into the music industry, but my hopes of becoming a success slowly began to fade when I realized that the recording, which I had done in 1970, was no longer being played on the radio, and was going nowhere. Even though I continued playing three nights a week in nightclubs and lounges, it became clear to me, after a while, that my dreams of becoming successful were fading rapidly. I was a failure. I just couldn't cut it in the music industry.

When facing failure, I always looked for someone else to blame, rather than me, and most of the time, I blamed my father. I hated him for abandoning his responsibilities and his family. His selfish, irresponsible actions had ultimately forced us to live in sheer poverty, in a two-room shack. My hatred for him intensified as I grew older, but at the same time, as ironic as it was, I despised the person I was becoming. I was a miserable young man and a failure – just like my father.

At the age of twenty-one, my life took a turn for the better when I met my future wife Trudy. She was a very young widow who tragically lost her first husband due to an alcohol-related, accidental death. Her husband was only eighteen years old at the time of his passing and she was left to fend for herself and her baby boy. Consequently, as we dated, it was understandable that she insisted that I quit my drinking before we could move into a serious relationship. It was difficult for us, but Trudy helped me to get free of the alcoholic lifestyle, and the misery and despair that always accompanied my addiction to alcohol. Because I loved her, my determination seemed to enable me to quit using alcohol, cold turkey. We did not know at the time that quitting an addiction for anyone or anything other than for oneself, will most often eventually end in failure.

A few months later, on August 25, 1973, Trudy and I were married. Our wedding took place on beautiful Church Island in the middle of Big Squam Lake, located in the popular Lakes Region of central New Hampshire. It was a beautiful, sunny, late summer day. My Uncle Frank, who was a Justice of the Peace, performed the ceremony, for a minimal fee. The only witnesses to our short ceremony were Trudy's parents.

At the time of our marriage, I was twenty-two years old, Trudy was twenty, and we became a happy little family. After we were married, we purchased some property with a house that we expected to live in for the rest of our lives. It was a beautiful piece of property with the best house in the neighborhood and was located only a few houses away from my mom's place, where I grew up. Our house was an old Cape Cod style house that had been built in the late 1800's. It had two big maple trees in front with a spacious lawn running down to the road. On the east side there was a beautiful garden, where we grew vegetables every summer. The wooded area behind the house extended up to the power line and was bordered with stone walls, which are commonly used in New England to set property lines. Our gravity-fed well, which was in the middle of the wooded section, provided us with cool, refreshing, clean water.

When we moved into our new home, we were both employed in factories – Trudy, in the town of Bristol and I, in the town of Ashland. We

IN THE WAR

worked long, hard hours. Each Monday through Saturday we began our days at 4:30 AM. Trudy was picked up at 5:00 AM and rode to work with neighbors, who were employed in the same factory, while I drove to the mill where I worked, and punched in at 6:00 AM.

Those were tiring days, but we were young and setting out on a new path, determined to climb the proverbial ladder of success. I was dead set on not being like my father. I thought this new beginning would bring peace, meaning and purpose to fill the void in my life. I did find love in my wife and children, which brought a measure of happiness, but ultimately, I was wrong. I found that my new lifestyle came up short and failed to fill the nagging emptiness in me. I remember often thinking: *Is this all there is to this life?* The constant, irritating emptiness led me to believe that there was nothing capable of quenching it – not even married life with children. Haunting, yet fundamental philosophical questions, which many people eventually ask, began percolating and racing through my mind and heart: *Who am I? Where am I going? What is my purpose in life? Why am I here? What happens to me when I die?* A terrible feeling of hopelessness was again rearing its ugly head.

It was during this time of questioning that we received a rather unexpected and surprising visitor one Saturday afternoon. Mr. Bush was my former music teacher in elementary school. As far back as I could remember, he was a very distinguished elderly man and one whom I highly respected. At the time of his visit, he would have been in his 80's. After meeting my wife and our two small boys he wasted no time in getting right to the point and the reason for his visit.

He began, "Robert," (he never called me Bob) "you have a beautiful wife and adorable children. You have a new car and a nice home. I have also been happy to notice, over these last few years, that your name is no longer in the court news." At this point, my face flushed with embarrassment as I realized that he was aware of my shameful past and numerous run-ins with the law. He continued, "I'm happy for you, and it looks like you've been able to turn your life around. However, I have come to tell you that you are lacking a relationship with God and His Son Jesus Christ.

43

I've come today to personally invite you and your family to join us in church tomorrow."

Though I respected Mr. Bush I said, "Thank you, but we are not really interested."

He smiled and said, "Well, you should come and hear the music. We have a young pastor and he and his wife sing beautiful duets."

The thought of a possible free concert intrigued me so I told him, "We will consider coming."

With that he thanked us and said, "Good, we will look forward to seeing you this Sunday morning at 11:00 AM."

We were not churchgoers, to say the least. I recall attending church with my nana on a couple of occasions, and as a little girl, Trudy went to an occasional Sunday School class. So, that was the extent of our knowledge of church.

On Sunday morning, we drove to the little community church, where we were warmly greeted by the pastor as we entered the sanctuary. We took our seats and listened to the opening remarks and Bible reading. The music was indeed beautiful. However, once the music was over and the pastor stood to preach his message, we got up out of the pew and headed for the doors. Over the next few weeks, we continued to go to church, but left after the musical portion of the service. One day the pastor called us and invited us to consider hearing one of his sermons. Eventually, we decided that perhaps we should stay and listen to the sermon. During the message, I became extremely intrigued with this Jesus he preached about. I remember saying to Trudy, "Either this guy has lost his mind, or he has something we're looking for."

After the service, Trudy and I discussed what we had heard and agreed that we should get our hands on a Bible and see what it was all about. Eventually, we purchased a Bible and immediately we had questions. We decided to ask the pastor for help, so without hesitation, we phoned him. "Reverend," I said, "this is Bob and Trudy, and we have a few questions about the Bible. Can you help us?"

44

IN THE WAR

After answering a couple of our questions, he said, "Bob, we are putting together a Bible study for new believers with a few other young couples like you and Trudy. Would you folks be interested in this study?"

I replied, "Yes!"

He continued, "We're also looking for a home to host this study, and perhaps you would feel more comfortable being in your own home – what do you think?"

"Well, who would be coming?" I asked. He named the individuals, some of whom we knew, and we agreed to have the study in our home, starting that fall in 1974.

The day of the first Tuesday night Bible study arrived, and we were excited! We had never hosted anything like this before and we certainly never had so many people coming to our home. It was our desire that all who attended would feel comfortable in our living room. Once Trudy and I had put the children to bed, we began getting everything ready for the meeting. We carefully arranged our living room to accommodate everyone and gathered as many ashtrays as we could find and placed them around the room. All of us, except the pastor and his wife, were smokers.

Pastor Everett and Pat were the first to arrive, followed by the others who were coming to the study.

The meeting began and so did the billowing of smoke. I remember seeing the pastor and his wife occasionally rubbing their eyes, during that first night. The smoke was thick, yet this devoted couple continued to teach us the Bible, and never uttered a single complaint. After a couple of weeks, once the pastor had arrived, I asked him if the smoke was too much for them. With a smile, he replied, "Well Bob, when the entire room gets blue with smoke it does make it a bit difficult."

I came back with what I thought was the perfect solution. I replied, "Everett, we can take smoke breaks out in the kitchen. Is that ok with you?"

45

BOB MCLAUGHLIN

He smiled and said, "Thank you, that's a wonderful solution."

Over the next few months, this faithful pastor and his wife led each one of us to a saving knowledge of Jesus Christ. I don't recall the actual date, but I do remember kneeling at my bed one day and praying to God. My prayer went something like this: "God, I am a sinner. Please forgive me for my many sins. Jesus, come into me and help me. Amen."

I told Trudy what I had done, and I could tell that she was so happy for me. She said, "I want to receive Jesus as well, but I want to make sure that I'm doing it for me and not just because you have done it." I knew this was a decision that she needed to make for herself without feeling pressured by my decision.

It wasn't long before Trudy knew what she had to do. In fact, it was the very next day when she made that most important decision and prayed to receive Jesus. We rejoiced over our new life and of course, we phoned our pastor with this very exciting news. One by one the others in the Bible study began surrendering to Jesus as well.

Several months later, in the summer of 1975, Pastor Everett baptized all fourteen members of the Tuesday night Bible study. How happy we were to belong to Jesus Christ, the Son of God, Who died for our sins on the cross, rose from the dead and now lived in us in all of His resurrection power.

That emptiness – the void, the vacuum previously in our lives was now filled with Jesus. Only God can provide a truly abundant life. Jesus said, "...*I came that they may have life, and have it abundantly.*" (John 10:10b NASB) Now we truly had found a new beginning!

IN THE WAR

Rev Everett Palmer Our Spiritual Father

Chapter 9

THE VISITOR

It was mid-afternoon on a Saturday in July 1975, and the day was hot and humid. Trudy and I were brand-new Christians, having given our lives to the Lord during the previous winter. Now we were looking forward to our baptismal service coming up in August. We were so excited about our newfound faith in Christ. Our walk with Jesus took top priority over everything. Church activities filled our evenings and our lives had become exciting and full of adventure. In fact, every day was new and thrilling, as our thirst for more knowledge of Jesus kept growing. Our intense desire to understand God's Holy Word led us to consume it with a ferocious appetite, so that we found ourselves spending large amounts of time studying and reading the Bible. It was not uncommon for us to be on the telephone with our dear Pastor Everett, asking him many questions and enthusiastically listening to his answers. We found that he was willing to answer all our questions and made it clear to us that any question was okay. He would accept our calls anytime that he was available, and he never displayed annoyance, even if it was a late-night call. His commitment and humility were amazing and hard to match.

Everett and Pat were not only our spiritual parents, but we had also become very close friends. We spent many days with them and even took vacations together. They loved us and our children, and we loved them. To this very day they remain our spiritual parents, and they continue to support us and our ministry. Admittedly, our biological families, who lived nearby, were very concerned and wondered if we had perhaps been brainwashed into a religious cult of some sort.

Trudy and I were in our kitchen on that hot July day when there was a knock on our door. I went to the door, opened it and there stood a young man. I assumed that he was a traveling salesman, so I said, "Hi, can we help you?" and invited him into our kitchen.

Once inside, he thanked us, smiled, and asked, "May I have a glass of water?"

I answered him without hesitating and with unusual exuberance, "Yes, of course!" I took a tall glass out of the cupboard, walked to the kitchen sink, and filled it from the faucet with cold, fresh water that came from our well. We watched with delight and satisfaction, as he quenched his thirst by drinking the entire glass of water.

When he finished, he handed the empty glass back to me, smiled, and said, "Thank you." I asked if he would like another, to which he replied, "No, thank you." He simply opened the door, said goodbye, and closed the door behind himself.

Once the door closed, we looked at each other and wondered the same thing: *Who was that? What just happened?* I recall that I said it out loud, "Who was that?" and then quickly opened the door. I was astonished to see that he was already gone. It was as if he had simply disappeared in a moment's time. I ran out through our enclosed porch and into our back yard. I frantically looked down the long dirt driveway, expecting to see an automobile making its way to the road but there was none. At that moment, it occurred to me that we hadn't heard a car drive up our long driveway, nor did our dog bark. Lassie never failed to raise the alarm with her barking whenever someone came onto our property. Furthermore, she was calmly lying down in her usual spot, right outside our porch.

IN THE WAR

My mind was battling the logistics of what had just happened. I knew that it would be impossible for our visitor to vacate our property on foot, or by car for that matter, in the amount of time that had elapsed since he closed our door. I mean, it was just a matter of seconds. I had run down our driveway to the road and looked both ways, but I saw no one. I had literally run all around the outside of our home, looking everywhere for this man, but He was nowhere to be found. Had he simply vanished without a trace? How could that be? There had to be a logical answer.

We called all our neighbors and described the man in detail to them, asking if they had seen anyone fitting that description. I asked whether they had perhaps seen a salesman at their door that day. Each neighbor replied that they had not seen anyone.

Then a sense of thrill filled my heart as I realized that Trudy and I were thinking the exact same thing. We wondered if it were possible that we had just entertained an angel! We were excited, to say the least, and yet at the same time, we couldn't help but wonder why God would send an angel to visit *us*. I mean, after all, who were we? We sat down and reviewed the entire event in detail from beginning to end. We concluded that, if God in His wisdom, decided to have one of His angels visit us, who were we to question His will? We humbly bowed in prayer and thanked the Lord Jesus for what we now considered to have been a divine appointment with one of God's angels. To this day, we wholeheartedly believe that we were blessed with a very special encounter with 'The Visitor.'

God tells us in the Bible, *"Do not neglect to show hospitality to strangers, for by this some have entertained angels without knowing it."* (Hebrews 13:2 NASB)

Chapter 10

THE CALL

The frail, slightly hunched old man shuffled along the streets of the quaint, classic New England town. His long white hair fluttered in the breeze from under the cap he wore. His hair, combined with his long white beard, gave him a most distinguished appearance. He wore old, round wire-rimmed glasses, perched on the end of his nose. He was indeed a spectacle. It was no surprise when children would often ask their concerned parents if this old man, living in their town, was Santa Claus. Young people mocked him. The adults said he has lost his mind. However, it was an unmistakable sight – he could be seen shuffling along with his cane and talking to himself. Erwin (not his real name) had become the talk of the town and provided much opportunity for dedicated gossipers.

Many of the locals had no idea where Erwin had spent the last fifty years of his life. Nor did they know all that he had accomplished. They were just convinced that he was 'off his rocker,' so to speak. They knew he was new in town and staying in a small apartment above the home of a retired minister, on Winter Street. In any small town, the old saying 'everybody knows everything about everybody' is mostly true. However, the people of this little New England 'mill town' could not have been more mistaken concerning this little old man.

Trudy and I heard the rumors about Erwin, and we were just as intrigued with him as were the other members of our small Bible study group. One Tuesday evening, during the study which we hosted in our home, someone asked Pastor Everett if he knew anything about the old man. Surprisingly, before he could answer the question, others began to blurt out unkind rumors that they had heard about him. The pastor sat silently, waiting patiently while this young, immature group finished sharing their 'insights.'

In hindsight, I'm sure Pastor Everett considered the fact that it was only several months earlier that he had led each of us to a saving knowledge of Jesus Christ, and then baptized us a few months after our conversion. We were all new to Christianity, so, to a degree, it was understandable that we would be eager to share everything we thought we knew about Erwin. Once the gossip stopped, Pastor Everett smiled and began to speak softly. However, before answering our question, he lovingly admonished us on the dangers of gossiping. We sheepishly sat through the remainder of the evening and listened as our trusted pastor told us the truth about this little old man.

It turned out that Erwin was not losing his mind, nor was he talking to himself as he walked around the small town. The truth was that this *little* old man was a *giant* man of God. Nearly every day he would walk around town, praying for all those who mocked him, those who thought he was losing his mind, and those who thought he was Santa Claus. He prayed for the entire community.

We were told that Erwin had come to town only a few months earlier, following the death of his dear wife. We were in awe to learn that she had died while serving as a missionary with her husband in Peru, South America. For fifty years they had ministered the Gospel of Jesus Christ to a tribal people group in the jungles of the eastern Amazon Basin. He was also an author and a gifted preacher of the Gospel. He and his wife had given those years of their lives to people that we hadn't even heard of until that evening.

IN THE WAR

At this point I was anxious to meet this interesting man of God. Little did I know then that it would not be long before we were to meet. More importantly, I was to discover that God would use Erwin to confirm His call on my life.

Trudy and I were so eager to grow in our new-found faith and knowledge of God that we spent much of our spare time reading God's Word and becoming active in several church activities. It was not uncommon for us to call our pastor with many immature questions. He would always take the time to answer us, no matter what he was doing when we called. He and his wife literally poured their lives into ours. We didn't know it was called 'discipleship' at that time, but discipling was exactly what they were doing. As a result of their ministry in our lives, we became involved in several church-related activities. We filled our free time with leading our little church's youth group, teaching Sunday school, and singing in the church choir. We loved serving and we were growing in leaps and bounds in our new faith in Christ.

One afternoon, while upstairs in our bedroom, kneeling in prayer beside our bed, I had an unusual awareness of the presence of God. In fact, the whole time spent in prayer that afternoon was very unusual and very intense. I knew something special was taking place. I had the Word of God open while I was praying. I remember reading about taking the Gospel to the world. I was praying fervently that God would allow us to do that. I remember saying to God, "I don't care to be famous, as some of the great preachers of the day, but please allow me to preach to as many people as they do." I vaguely recall thinking, *what a foolish prayer to pray,* but it was at that moment that I thought I heard God speak to me. It was not an audible voice, but it was as clear as an audible voice would be. I was awestruck. I was stunned! Could it really be possible that God had just spoken to me? Was it God, or was it something else? I had to find out the truth.

BOB MCLAUGHLIN

I ran downstairs and shared with Trudy what I believed God had just said to me. She was amazed, but also wondered if it really was God speaking. We both agreed that we needed to talk to a mature Christian, but we were unable to contact Pastor Everett – I think he was out of town at the time. However, this was so important to us that it just could not be set aside for long. Though immature and impatient, we set out to discover the truth about what had happened. We prayed for God to lead us to someone who could be trusted; someone who could tell us if this was of God or just something I had imagined. Erwin came to mind and we both agreed that we should contact this dear man right away. I called him and arranged for a meeting.

Anticipation and excitement ran high as we drove several miles into town. We parked outside the one-hundred-year-old house, which sported a classic white clapboard exterior, and with our two young boys in tow, we climbed the stairs to a little apartment. We knocked on the door. It flew open and there stood Erwin, the talk of the town. Peering through his wire-rimmed glasses, his warm eyes gave us the distinct impression that he was smiling under his white beard. With a soft and inviting voice, he welcomed us into his little home. The simple apartment comprised a tiny kitchen, a bathroom and a bedroom. Though it was small and sparsely furnished, it was warm and cozy. He gave the boys some cookies and milk.

It soon became clear to us that our young boys were unable to hide their obvious curiosity. They sat and stared wide-eyed at this dear old saint. Finally, unable to keep it in any longer, our son Joshua said to him, "You look like Santa!"

Erwin chuckled and leaned over to Trudy and me and said, "The 'n' is in the wrong place." It took us a moment, but we finally understood what he meant: he viewed Santa as a tool of Satan, robbing us of the true meaning of Christmas.

He then made us some tea, thanked us for calling him and got right to the point, asking us what advice we wanted. Erwin

IN THE WAR

remained silent, while staring at my face and carefully watching my body language. I admit I was a bit uncomfortable. I felt as if he could see right through me. It was an odd sensation, sitting there, in front of this saint. In fact, I remember thinking that it was like I was talking to a man who resembled a Biblical character, like Moses. Yet we knew he was listening to my every word and sensed that God had arranged this very important meeting.

I shared what I believed had happened while I was reading God's Word and praying in my bedroom. I told him about my prayer. Still, he remained silent. I gathered some confidence and gingerly said, "I think God spoke to me after I prayed that prayer!" At that point, his eyes squinted as he leaned in closer to my face. I felt like I was under very close examination and became even more uncomfortable.

It was then that he said these words, "Tell me exactly what you think God said, young man. Don't leave anything out. Tell me every word He said."

Though I had no intention of stretching or embellishing what I felt God had said to me, I was still afraid. I knew it was very important that what I shared with Erwin would be accurate and complete. I repositioned myself ever so slightly, as if I was attempting to move out from underneath his steely eyes, which seemed to pierce through the wire-rimmed glasses, and mercilessly cut deep into my frightened soul. I prayed silently, asking the Lord to carefully guide my words. As I took a deep breath and started repeating what I strongly believed God had said to me that afternoon, the words seemed to fall boldly from my lips. I heard myself saying, "God said these words to me after my prayer that day. He said, 'I am going to use you in a powerful and mighty way...'" At that point I paused, just like God had done. Erwin's face contorted with an obvious look of deep concern as I paused before finishing the sentence. I locked eyes with him again, and then continued with

57

BOB MCLAUGHLIN

the rest of what God had said, "'...but, not without a lot of trials and tribulations!'"

I was astonished, yet greatly relieved, at what happened next. Erwin sat upright in his chair and his face lit up. He thrust his hand forward and grabbed my shoulder, saying, "That's of God, young man!! That's of God!!" I wanted to shout with joy when he affirmed my belief that the message I had received was indeed from God. Admittedly, I was excited about the first half of His message, but I was not too happy with the second part. Who in their right mind would want lots of trials and tribulations in their life? Yet, somehow, we knew this was our future – that had been confirmed. In the coming years we would see just how accurate that message would be. Now, some forty-two years later, we can testify, without hesitation, that God had truly spoken those words to me that day.

Before leaving Erwin's home, he laid hands on us and offered what we now know was a prophetic prayer. He bid us good day and I left with his words repeatedly ringing loudly and clearly in my mind: *That's of God, young man!! That's of God!!* As we went to bed that evening, we really had no idea what the future would hold. We just knew that God's message to me would be foundational for our future.

Chapter 11

A FLEDGLING EVANGELIST

When Trudy and I became Christians, several months after our wedding, our entire focus on life and the purpose for our existence totally changed. For example, in my teen years, when I was playing in a Rock and Roll band, my world centered around music and my dreams of making it big in the secular music business. When our band broke up, and I later quit playing in the nightclubs and lounges, my hopes and dreams died. Now, my goal of being successful in secular music quickly changed to a desire to use my musical abilities for the Lord in the church.

We just wanted to live for Jesus, and we thought that serving the Lord would simply mean serving Him in our small, local, Baptist church. We were quite content with the idea of continuing to live in our little area of New Hampshire. At the time, we had no idea just how big the Lord's plans were for us.

There were two very memorable incidents, which took place early in my new walk with Jesus, that were fundamental in my growth as a Christian and my future calling as an evangelist. As mentioned in an earlier chapter, I had read in the Bible about taking the good news to others and had prayed that God would allow us to do that.

The first incident took place shortly after our conversion and baptism. Trudy and I were Christmas shopping in the small strip mall in west Plymouth. I was looking for a tool type of gift for my brother John. We entered a hardware store and while we were looking over the various potential tools, a young man walked through the door and came right up to us. With a winning smile and his hand extended to shake my hand, he said, "Bob McLaughlin, how are you?" I immediately recognized him. We had attended High School at the same time and did a fair amount of drinking together, in past years.

I responded with a firm handshake and said, "Oh my, it's you, John! This is my wife Trudy. It's been a few years since I saw you last. I am fine, how are you?"

He said, "I'm not doing so well." I asked him what he meant, and he replied, "The doctor tells me I have a bad heart."

I responded in surprise with, "What? How can that be? You cannot be more than twenty-five years old, right?"

John replied, "Yeah that is right, but listen. I understand your life has changed. Would you please share your new life with me? I'm interested and want to know what happened."

I stood there in disbelief and stared silently at him for a moment or two. At the same time, the fear of possible rejection gripped my heart. Yet, here for the first time since my conversion to Christ, someone was asking me to share about what it was that changed my life. To my great shame I chose, as an act of my will, to lie straight-faced to John and said, "John, listen, the holidays are upon us, and I have a meeting I have to go to. But once the holiday season is over, I will call you in the New Year and we will go out for a coffee, and I will share with you how my life has changed."

John smiled and said, "OK, I really want to know, so please do call me after the holidays." With the same winning smile and another handshake, he said goodbye.

IN THE WAR

I was relieved as John left the store that day. Yet as I watched him walk away, an annoying feeling of guilt, which I attempted to ignore, welled up in my heart. I reasoned that, though I lied to him, I had made plans to meet with him in just a few days.

Now that we were Christians, Christmas took on a totally different meaning and focus. All those Christmas carols we sang as children, now made total sense to us as we realized that Jesus is the real reason for the season. It was now all about Jesus and less about us. It truly had become a beautiful time of the year when we, as Christians, could celebrate the birth of our Lord and Savior, Jesus Christ.

Christmas Eve came, and our excitement rose as we bundled up our young family and drove to the church for a beautiful candlelight service. The church was full, and the sound of everyone singing beautiful Christmas carols blending with the soft candlelight brought tears to my eyes. As we drove home, following the service, my heart was filled with joy and thankfulness for our new life in Christ. Once we got home we prayed with the children and put them to bed. Trudy and I sat in our living room admiring the soft colorful lights illuminating from our beautiful Christmas tree, with all the wrapped gifts under it. To add to our joy, a gentle snow was falling, assuring us of a perfect and classic New Hampshire white Christmas. What could be better?

Christmas morning came early, and our children were excited. Their excitement was contagious, and they just could not wait to open their gifts. We all went to the living room and the first thing we did was to sing happy birthday to Jesus. We watched with great joy as our two little boys unwrapped their gifts. We enjoyed a wonderful Christmas dinner and sang a few Christmas carols. It was truly a most wonderful day. I remember going to bed, later that evening, rejoicing in my heart that God had sent His Son to earth to pay the price for my salvation.

BOB MCLAUGHLIN

The next day our telephone rang. My mom phoned to ask if I had heard about John. I questioned mom – thinking, wondering what happened to my brother John. My mom said, "No Robby, not your brother John, I'm talking about your friend John M."

I responded, "Yes, I just saw him a few days ago and guess what Mom? He wants to know how and why my life has changed. I will be calling him in the New Year, and we are going out for coffee, and I am going to share Jesus with him. Isn't that great Mom?"

Mom was silent for a moment before responding, "Robby, John died on Christmas Day."

I replied, "WHAT?"

Mom repeated, "John died on Christmas Day." My brain and body went numb. The first thing that hit me was disbelief, followed by a hope that what I was hearing was not true. John, dead? I was just talking with him a few days ago – how could this be? Of all the days, he died on Christmas Day! While I was rejoicing over my new life in Christ, John was dying. I do not recall how my conversation with my mom ended. I guess I was just in shock.

After a day or two I found out about the last few minutes of his life. I was told that, at the time of his death, there was only one person with him in his hospital room. John's sister sat by his bed, held his trembling hand and witnessed his last words before dying. With fear in his eyes, he looked at her and said, "I'm afraid to die," and breathed his last breath and entered eternity.

Just a few days before John's passing, that young man stood before me and asked me to share my new life with him. However, as an act of my will, I deliberately lied to him, choosing, out of fear, to not share Christ with him that day.

Over the years, he remains the only person who has approached me and directly asked me to share about my new life. There is a story in the book of Acts, where an earthquake broke open a jail, loosening all the prisoners, including Paul and Silas. The frightened jailer then asked them, *"'Sirs, what must I do to be saved?'"* (Acts

IN THE WAR

16:30 NASB) When I read this passage, guess who comes to mind? My encounter with John is the closest anyone has ever come to just outright asking me, "What must I do to be saved?"

It took me a long time to fully accept God's forgiveness for my failure to share Jesus with John that day. The shame and guilt weighed heavy on me. I felt his blood was on my hands. Thankfully, over time and with counseling from my pastor, the guilt and shame gradually dispersed. Now I am forgiven, and I am cleansed. However, I learned the hard way that I must take advantage of every opportunity to share Christ with the lost.

The second memorable event involved my family. When one becomes a Christian, often some of the first people they desire to share the good news with are, of course, their family members. As new Christians, this was our desire.

Since we lived in the same neighborhood as my mom, she helped with babysitting our two small boys while we were at work. My brother John and his family had purchased a home in nearby Plymouth, so they were often at my mom's house as well. This situation provided many opportunities to be with my family. Because of our desire to share with them, we would often talk about our involvement in the church and our new Christian family.

Eventually, I decided it was time to share the gospel with my brother John. As mentioned earlier, John and I had a strained relationship, and ever since Trudy and I had been converted to Christ, his antagonism had intensified towards us, as well as our new friends and the church in general. I felt that his bitterness towards me was due to all the trouble I had brought on our mom and his family during my drinking years. It was John who bailed me out of jail more times than I care to remember. Though I would often attempt to express my sincere appreciation for the many sacrifices he made on my behalf, it would usually quickly decline into some form of an argument.

63

Finally, what I thought was an opportune time to confront him with the gospel, had arrived. I do not recall exactly how we got into our conversation that day, but it was usually a result of John making a wisecrack about our new life. So here is what I do remember.

John and I were standing, facing each other, in our mom's kitchen. As the conversation intensified, I remember saying, "John, God loves you. He loves you so much that Jesus, God's Son, came to earth and died on the cross for your sins, and on the third day He rose from the dead – therefore we celebrate things like Christmas and Easter. It's all about Jesus."

It is important to understand that John knew every button to push, to bring me to a point of rage. He had perfected this art of antagonism over the years. He knew I had a temper – like my father. He knew I could fly off the handle very quickly. And to my shame, he had witnessed my temper tantrums many times during my childhood and drunken teenage years.

Soon our conversation turned into one of our typical arguments. Sadly, this evangelistic witnessing opportunity became a shouting match. John skillfully waited for the perfect time to start jabbing his finger into my chest, just inches from my face, and shouting, "WHAT DO YOU WANT ME TO DO, ROBBY?"

In an instant, rage overtook me, and I extended my arm behind me and swung at him as hard as I could, slapping him right across his face, while at the same time, shouting, "REPENT! THAT IS WHAT I WANT YOU TO DO!"

For a few moments the silence was deafening. Everyone who was present displayed a look of utter disbelief at what had just happened. John looked at me, a bit shocked, yet there was also a hint of satisfaction in his eyes as he said with a smirk, "No thanks, I don't think I want to become one of you."

Guilt and shame washed over me. Nothing further was said and we went home. Over and over I would ask myself, and cry out to the Lord with the question, *Why would I do such a thing?* The enemy came down hard on me with, *Way to go Bob! Some evangelistic meeting that was.* I honestly thought I would never live this one down; I had failed the Lord so badly. I failed in sharing the love of Jesus. I mean, really, what love was there in that slap? Clearly this was not a successful witnessing experience! Of course, I repented and eventually apologized, but I was sure John would never give his heart to Jesus, and that it would be because of me.

Trudy and I prayed frequently for our extended families. We prayed that, despite knowing who I had been and the many terrible things I had done, God would somehow and in some way draw each of them to Himself.

Many things happened over the next few years: being accepted and involved in full-time ministry; the sale of our home; a ministry in Washington, DC for two years; and a huge move across the continent to Abbotsford, British Columbia.

It was when we were back in New Hampshire, on one of our annual reporting and preaching circuits, that an amazing turn of events took place. It was truly a God-orchestrated event.

I was scheduled to preach in a Baptist church in Ashland – one of our supporting churches. The pastor gave me the Sunday morning service to give a brief report and to deliver the morning sermon. Trudy and I, along with our four children, drove into a parking lot near the church. As we were getting out of our car, I was surprised to see my brother John, his family, and my mom parked right beside us. As John got out of his car he said, with a smirk on his face, "I thought we would come and hear the preacher this morning. I read in the paper that he was going to be preaching here today. Don't worry. We are going to sit right in the front pews and give this preacher a listen."

I found this hard to believe, but replied, "Good, we are glad that you are here."

That morning the church was totally full. As promised, my brother and his family, along with my mom, sat right at the front of the sanctuary. As the service began, I prayed that the Holy Spirit would move during the service and that many would find true salvation in Christ, and I especially prayed for my family members.

I stood to preach, and I sensed the presence of the Holy Spirit. The service seemed to be electrified with the power of God Almighty. I was able to preach a simple, straightforward, evangelistic message with unusual authority. Amazingly, I was not intimidated by John's presence. At the end of my message, I extended a public invitation for any who wanted to repent of their sins and receive Jesus, to come forward and stand at the front of the church. To my utter amazement, more than thirty people came forward, many in tears. In the very front and standing side by side, were the first ones to come forward: my brother John, his wife Brenda, their three daughters and my dear mom. Glory to God! My prayers through all those years had been answered.

The Bible says, *"The Lord is not slow about His promise, as some count slowness, but is patient toward you, not wishing for any to perish but for all to come to repentance."* (2 Peter 3:9 NASB) God's timing is perfect.

The first story shows how I totally failed God by letting fear take over and keep me from speaking up when He gave me the opportunity to witness for Him. I did make plans to talk with John M. later, but I deliberately didn't obey when I was faced with his questions. It was a hard way to learn the lesson that obedience to God needs to come when He says so, and not be put off for another time.

In the second story, I did try to obey God when I felt it was time, but I did it in my own way and ended up in a shouting match with my brother. Fortunately, the story didn't end there, and I didn't give up, but continued to pray for my family. After several years had passed and I was given the opportunity to speak to them from the pulpit, God gave me a message which I preached through the power of the Holy Spirit. This time I obeyed God and saw Him work in the lives of my family.

IN THE WAR

The lesson I have learned is that it is important for me to obey God and tell people about Him whenever they cross my path, and then to leave the results to Him. These two stories of 'evangelizing' clearly illustrate that I was just a 'fledgling evangelist' during my early walk with Jesus, but now evangelism is my full-time ministry. Obedience to God has taken me from failure to amazing opportunities to preach all over the world. God just wants us to be obedient and willing to be used by Him. Is there someone God has brought to your mind, whom you need to share Christ with? I encourage you to obey God and do it.

PART THREE
EARLY MINISTRY

Chapter 12

CAMPUS CRUSADE FOR CHRIST

All the small towns in the Lakes Region of central New Hampshire were electric with excitement. For many months, the area churches had been actively involved in preparation for an evangelistic crusade that was coming to the area.

Trudy and I, along with a good number of other folks, received counselor training which was needed for the initial follow-up with those who would receive Christ during the crusade. Though we were young in our faith, we were encouraged by our pastor and others in our church to get actively involved because, as they said, "You will receive a blessing." They were right.

The crusade advance set-up person, Mr. Howard, made several trips to our area to make sure things were lining up properly for the event. He stressed the essential need for all the churches to be fervently praying for the crusade. He said prayer was critical to the success of any effort in reaching the lost with the gospel. So, prayer meetings were set up all over our communities.

I was excited and honored to have joined a weekly lunch hour prayer meeting consisting of several pastors and other concerned Christians. The meeting took place in the town of Plymouth at the home of a crusade committee member.

During one of Mr. Howard's visits to the area, he chose to attend the prayer meeting I was participating in. I was impressed with his deep desire to see our area reap a great harvest of souls for the Kingdom of God. I was surprised when, following the meeting, he approached me and asked if he could take me out for lunch the next day. I could hardly believe that, of all the people he could meet with, he chose to meet with me.

At this time, I was working in the headquarters of the power company located in West Plymouth. The morning of the day we were to meet for lunch seemed to go by quickly. All morning I was anticipating and wondering why such a person like Mr. Howard would want to meet with me. I admit that I was excited, yet I felt unworthy for such a meeting.

We met at the scheduled time and place, took a booth in the small restaurant, and ordered our lunch. Following all the basic opening conversational pleasantries, Mr. Howard dove right in and asked me if I would share my personal testimony with him. I was happy to accommodate his request and commenced to do so. As I was sharing my testimony it was obvious to me that he was listening intently to every word I was sharing. When I finished, he smiled, looked into my eyes, and asked, "Bob, what do you really want to do with your life?"

I was a bit taken aback with his direct question but found myself answering, "I want to serve the Lord full time, but I do not think that would be possible."

"Why, Bob?" he asked.

The reason I said that was because, only a few months earlier, we had applied with a mission organization and were flatly turned down. So, at this point I decided to tell Mr. Howard about our experience.

I told him how we had attended a special evening service at our church to hear a missionary couple report on their ministry in New Guinea. They spoke with enthusiasm while they presented an

IN THE WAR

amazing slideshow of their jungle ministry. Consequently, when I saw their presentation, my heart leaped, and I was sure we were going to New Guinea to be missionaries. Trudy, on the other hand, was not so sure. Reluctantly, however, Trudy agreed to fill out the application forms and we sent them in. I relayed how our pastor lovingly tried to inform me that, perhaps, it was a bit premature of me to assume God was leading us to be missionaries. I thanked him for his concern and assured him that I was more than convinced we would be accepted. Well, I could not have been more wrong. A few weeks later we received a nice letter from the mission stating that, though they were sure God has a plan for us, it would not be as missionaries with their organization. I talked about how crushed I was, to say the least. How could I have misunderstood this whole thing? What did God want to teach me? Then I explained how I learned that they were right, and God did have a perfect plan for us. It turned out that the rejection helped us to make a major decision. It became clear to us that we needed to further our education and, in order to do that, we went back to high school. Both Trudy and I were high school dropouts and there we were, at our age, going back to school. We attended evening classes for several months at the Plymouth High School and obtained our high school equivalency diplomas.

Now, as I am writing this and looking back at those days, the whole thing seems quite laughable. I was twenty-five years old, and Trudy was twenty-three. I was so immature and bullheaded (Trudy would say I still have some of that), but we certainly had tenacity!

Meanwhile, Mr. Howard had sat, grinning, through my entire testimony. When I finished, he asked, "Bob, what do you enjoy doing?"

I answered, "I enjoy making music for the Lord."

Mr. Howard continued by asking me another question, "Bob, do you know that the Lord can use you in full time music ministry?"

"Really? How so?" I asked.

BOB MCLAUGHLIN

Still smiling, he reached into his briefcase, pulled out a magazine and as he slid it across the table he asked, "Have you ever heard of Campus Crusade for Christ?"

I replied, "No."

He continued, "This is a copy of the *Worldwide Challenge* magazine published by Campus Crusade. Bob, I want to give you this magazine for you and Trudy to read. Campus Crusade for Christ is looking for young Christians like you to help fulfill the Great Commission. You guys would fit right in with them. Take it home with you and when you are ready, cut out the info clipping, send it in to them and let's see what happens." I thanked him and he asked if he could pray for us. We bowed our heads together and he prayed for God to guide and direct us and to bless our future ministry. Although we didn't know it at the time, it was a prophetic prayer. As we parted, he said, "Bob, God has an exciting plan for you and your family."

I took the magazine home and we read through it entirely. After we had taken some time to pray, we sent in the clipping requesting more information and an application form. This was when we depended on the Post Office for mail service, so it took a couple of weeks before we received the requested papers. Once they did arrive, we didn't fill them out right away. We were still a bit skittish due to the rejection we had received from the other mission, so the application form remained blank, lying on our dresser for a few weeks.

However, God works in mysterious ways!

When my employment with the power company came to an abrupt and unexpected end, I went home and told Trudy I had just lost my job and that I was going to the church to pray. After I drove several miles to get to the church, I walked in and sat silently in the front pew for a few minutes. I bowed my head and prayed for wisdom. I asked the Lord to show me what I should do. What happened next was nothing short of His clear intervention.

74

I walked up to the pulpit and just as I looked down at the incredibly large, old, pulpit Bible, the sun shone through the large, colorful, church window just behind me and the rays of sunlight fell on the open Bible. The passage of scripture that was suddenly illuminated by the sun's rays on it was Proverbs 3:5-6. *"Trust in the LORD with all thine heart; and lean not unto thine own understanding. In all thy ways acknowledge Him, and He shall direct thy paths."* (KJV) In that moment I knew God had directed me to *that* church and to *that* passage at *that* very moment to show me His power to answer our prayers. Just think! God's timing was perfect in arranging the sun to shine through the window and directly illuminate that passage of scripture just when I was standing in the pulpit. That moment was surreal, and I was affirmed by my God that He would take care of us.

I went home and told Trudy what had happened. We immediately sat down together and filled out the Campus Crusade for Christ (CCC) application. Within a day or two we mailed it to Arrowhead Springs in San Bernardino, California where the Campus Crusade headquarters were located.

While we waited to see how God was going to lead us, I was able to get a job at a grocery market in Plymouth. The pay was little, but we were thankful for the employment. Before long, we received a call from a Campus Crusade staff member who was ministering at the University of New Hampshire (UNH). He wanted to set up a convenient time for a formal interview. We agreed on a date and then asked all our friends at church to pray for us.

The anticipated evening came, and two Campus Crusade staff members arrived at our home to conduct the official interview. The leader was the Campus Crusade director at UNH, and he was accompanied by his assistant. We found them to be so kind and we immediately felt comfortable with them. After we opened in prayer, the interview began, and it went off without a hitch. They told us we would most likely be invited to the annual four-week Institute of Biblical Studies, which would be held in Fort Collins, Colorado. If we were accepted on staff, we would remain for another two weeks for the staff training and conference.

I remember asking how much it would cost for our family to fly to Denver. He asked me what airline I would prefer to fly with. That was easy to answer because we had never flown before and TWA was the only airline company that I was aware of. He picked up our phone, called TWA and gave us the cost. He also said that there would be other expenses for which we would have to trust the Lord to supply.

A few days later we received an official invitation to attend the Institute of Biblical Studies, taught by the International School of Theology, at the Colorado State University in Fort Collins, Colorado. Classes would begin in June, and we needed to raise about $1,800.00 to cover flights and the other expenses. We were very excited, to say the least.

Our church and Christian friends began making donations for our ministry training and we were amazed at how quickly the needs were met for our upcoming summer adventure. Our flights were booked and on June 9, 1978, our pastor, Everett Palmer, drove our family of five to Boston's Logan airport. On our arrival at the airport, he prayed for us and read Joshua 1:9: *"Have I not commanded you? Be strong and courageous! Do not tremble or be dismayed, for the Lord your God is with you wherever you go."* (NASB)

Trudy and I were indeed country bumpkins who had never flown on an airplane nor been west of the state of Vermont; so, this was a big deal for us. We were thrilled to even think that God could possibly use us in an organization the size of Campus Crusade for Christ.

We arrived at Stapleton International airport in Denver, Colorado and were met by some genuinely nice CCC staff who drove us to the Fort Collins Colorado State University Campus. We were assigned to Corbett Hall and given two rooms – side by side

IN THE WAR

with a connecting door. Once we got settled, we ventured outside onto the campus with our three children and began to mingle with the others. Hundreds of staff and potential staff had converged on the campus, so the place was buzzing with many young people and a good number of families like ours.

Trudy and I got little sleep that first night because we were so excited and more than a little anxious, knowing that the next day was registration and orientation. Fortunately, our children slept well, considering they were in a totally different environment. That morning we felt ready to tackle whatever the day would bring.

We got dressed and headed off to breakfast in the huge dining hall. Following breakfast, we dropped our children off at the make-shift daycare which was conveniently set up on campus. The staff who took care of the children were amazing and made us feel at ease about leaving them in their care.

Next, we dug out the campus map and made our way to registration, which turned out to be an absolute hoot. I wish you could have been there to witness how it all went down. Trudy and I walked into this huge hall where there were hundreds of young people lined up to register, the majority of whom were the cream of the crop of academia. This was the setting: Campus Crusade staff sat behind several long tables pushed together to make one very long extended table to accommodate the masses. In front of each staff person was a large piece of paper taped to the edge of the table with a large letter on it. We were to line up in front of the paper with the letter that matched the first letter of our last name. Trudy and I lined up in the 'M' line and waited for our turn to register. As we approached the table, the young man sitting there reached over to a pile of registration forms, looked up at us with a pleasant smile and said, "May I have your names and address please?" I responded by answering his question. While he was writing, I smiled to myself, thinking that this wasn't going to be so hard after all – I had done this kind of thing every time I was arrested by the police. He jotted down the information on the registration form and asked us the next question, "OK, now, what university?"

I responded with, "What do you mean?"

He replied, "Well, I am asking you which university you graduated from?"

I said, "Oh, OK, well we did not graduate from any university."

He looked up at me and asked, "Well then, what college did you graduate from?"

I looked at him with a bit of a smile and said, "Well, we did not graduate from a college either." Then before he could respond to my answer, I said with a big smile, "But we do have our high school equivalency diplomas!"

The look on his face was priceless, to say the least. He readjusted his contorted face and managed an awkward smile as he slowly emphasized, "OK!" and then continued, "So when did you graduate and receive your equivalency diplomas?"

Still smiling, I answered, "Well you see, we did not really have a graduation ceremony per se; we simply received our diplomas in the mail." It was fun seeing his reaction as I gave my answers to each of his questions – he would kind of tip his head ever so slightly and his smile grew broader and broader.

When we eventually finished registering, he thanked us and said, "Welcome to the Institute of Biblical Studies." We thanked him and as we walked away, I glanced back and saw him looking up and smiling to himself. Now, many years later, as we look back on the situation, Trudy and I laugh, thinking he was probably wondering: *How on earth did those guys make it through the screening process?*

Those four weeks of training were indeed a challenge for us. The professors were kind to us in grading our papers and exams, but they quickly recognized, and were more interested in, our hearts' strong desire to serve the Lord.

I was once again filled with anxiety as the day came for my audition for the Campus Crusade music ministry. Trudy and I sat

IN THE WAR

in front of a semicircle of 'music majors,' who made up the committee that would decide if I was cut out for the music ministry. In the center of this committee sat the CCC national director of music ministry.

After we greeted one another, I was told to audition with my guitar. I was nervous but played well. They asked if I could read music, to which I answered that I used to as a kid but that I'd since forgotten how and simply played by ear now.

Then the national director looked at Trudy and asked her the following question, "Trudy, what do you think about Bob being away from you and the children while ministering on international trips, some of which will be up to a month long?"

My dear Trudy squared off with him, leaned forward with her eyes squinting ever so slightly, stared at him and said with a somewhat elevated and raspy voice, "I would not like that one bit!" The blood drained immediately from my face, and I almost fell out of my chair. My head began to spin as I thought: *Well, there goes the opportunity to be with Campus Crusade.* I attempted to compose myself and was surprised when the whole committee appeared to agree with her – through their smiles of approval. I was not impressed. In fact, I was a bit angry at her honesty.

The audition ended and they said, "If you are accepted on staff, then we will let you know if you can be in the music ministry."

The walk back to our dorm was tense. Trudy told me, in no uncertain terms, "Either God will arrange for you to never have to leave me and the children to go on tours or, He will change my heart – and He won't change my heart about this!" I knew she was serious and frankly, I thought this could make or break the idea of being in a touring music ministry. She agreed that we should pray much about this, and we did.

As the time approached when the personnel department, through much prayer, had to decide who would be accepted on staff and who would be rejected, we became more and more anxious.

We had developed amazing friendships; especially with those who were in the same dormitory. They all assured us that we would be accepted.

I remember the last day when the final decision had to be made. The later it got the more our anxiety increased. While we waited for the final decision, we met with some friends in the common area right next to our room and prayed. Those who gathered with us were either current staff or had already been accepted. We were the last in our dorm still waiting to get the call from personnel with their decision. Through the open door, we finally heard our telephone ring. I ran to answer the phone. As I recall, it was about 9:00 PM when the call came. The gentleman on the other end introduced himself as the director of the Campus Crusade for Christ personnel department and asked how we were holding up. I answered, "Well sir, we are good, and we are waiting for your decision."

"Bob," he said, "You and Trudy caused us a sleepless night last night. We were praying all night and all today for God's wisdom, and He has answered us. We are happy to inform you that you and your family have been officially accepted as Campus Crusade staff, and therefore you will remain here for another two weeks for staff training." I was overjoyed and thanked him profusely. He continued, "May God bless you and welcome to the Campus Crusade for Christ family."

After hanging up the phone, I ran out of our room to where everyone was looking questioningly at me. I shouted, "We have been accepted on staff!" Our friends hugged us, and we all shed tears of joy as cries of "Praise God!" and "Hallelujah!" were heard. Then we bowed our heads and prayed, thanking God for the guidance He had given to the Campus Crusade leadership.

When we finished praying, a young couple handed me the keys to their little Volkswagen and said, "We'll watch the kids, you guys just go out and celebrate." We were beside ourselves with excitement. We drove to a Kentucky Fried Chicken and celebrated over

IN THE WAR

some chicken and fries. We could hardly believe that we were on staff with Campus Crusade for Christ. The four weeks we had just gone through were a real blessing and we had made some amazing friendships.

Staff training was yet another challenge. We had to memorize the CCC evangelistic booklet *The Four Spiritual Laws* and attend many different meetings.

We did receive word that I had been approved for the music ministry. I was assigned to the Washington, DC music group called Great Commission Company and I would be the only guitarist. By now the Holy Spirit had been tenderly working on my Trudy. Her heart was softening as she realized this was, indeed, God's calling.

The end of staff conference and training came, and it was time for us to meet Dr. and Mrs. Bill Bright. A huge banquet was held, followed by a reception line for all new staff to meet and greet the founders of Campus Crusade, Dr. Bill, and Vonette Bright. As I was shaking Dr. Bright's hand, I said, "Dr. Bright, it's an honor to meet you." He smiled and welcomed me on staff.

As I was greeting Mrs. Bright, I heard Trudy say, as she grabbed Dr. Bright's hand, "Hi Bill, I'm Trudy and how are you?"

He laughed and said, "I am fine, Trudy, and welcome to Campus Crusade."

Now that staff training was finished, we flew back to Boston where we were met by Pastor Everett and his wife Pat, who drove us home. We began the huge task of trusting God for our support needs, selling our home and property so we could move to Fairfax, Virginia, and then finding a new home. There was so much to do!

After we sold our home we rented a two-room cabin while we waited, trusting the Lord to provide the funds for our new ministry – $1,836.00 per month. Back in 1978 that was a lot of support to raise in central New Hampshire, but our God was faithful, and He provided the resources.

81

My first international tour was to Yugoslavia and Romania in the spring of 1979. While I was away for the thirty-three days, Trudy and the children remained in New Hampshire. God was faithful! First, He changed Trudy's heart, and then He took care of her and the children during my absence.

Bob in music ministry

Chapter 13

MINISTRY BEGINS

In the summer of 1979, once we had raised all the support we needed, we made the move to Fairfax, Virginia and rented an apartment. Our ministry had begun, and it was so exciting!

We served a year and a half in Virginia. In early 1980, we were informed that the DC music ministry was being shut down. We were told to pray about choosing to be relocated either to southern California or the greater Vancouver, British Columbia, Canada area. After much prayer and counseling we made the decision to join the music ministry in British Columbia.

We rented a small U-Haul, packed up our belongings and drove 3,200 miles across the United States to British Columbia. At last our family of six, including Becky, our fourth child, who was only two weeks old at the time of our move, arrived at the Canadian border. The Canadian office of CCC made all the arrangements plus sent some staff to meet us, so when we arrived at the Aldergrove border crossing I was able to pick up my work visa and enter Canada. From 1980 to 1982 I was the guitarist with the Canadian music group called Forerunner. Later, I joined the Here's Life ministry of CCC, conducting evangelism training seminars in churches in British Columbia.

BOB MCLAUGHLIN

A year or so after arriving in Canada, and after much prayer and the encouragement of the Canadian staff, we decided to apply for landed immigrant status. Eventually, issues regarding our application caused a serious turn of events.

The application had involved lengthy and detailed questions, some of which related to my past with law authorities in New Hampshire. These questions had concerned me because I was not sure I was answering them accurately, due to the condition I was in each time I was arrested and the span of years since those convictions took place. Because our lives had been dramatically changed when we received Christ, and total transparency and honesty were therefore important to us, we found ourselves in a dilemma regarding the details on the application. At the time, we decided that the best way to solve this dilemma was to obtain all my police records and submit them, with a cover letter of explanation, along with the application to the Canadian consulate.

I flew back east and collected my records from the police and sheriff's departments. The clerk at the front desk began photocopying my records for me, as well as taking time to read through them. He asked, "So, what is it you do now?" I told him that I was in full-time ministry of the gospel of Christ. The look of surprise on his face was priceless, especially since he had just read through my records which described, in detail, each arrest, including all of my colorful quotes that I screamed. Next, he asked me, "What do you plan to do with these records?" I explained my circumstances and what my plan was. Smirking, he said, "Good luck with that, buddy." I thought it was the only way to handle this situation and I thought I would be commended for being so honest. I later realized that although being honest is good for the soul, it's not always good for the reputation.

Once I got back home, I drafted a cover letter of explanation and sent in my application. I was confident we would be accepted right away. I was dead wrong again! A few days later I received a

IN THE WAR

call from the border crossing in Aldergrove. They requested that I come for a meeting on the upcoming Friday. I was excited and asked, "Is this regarding our landed immigrant status?"

They answered, "Yes, it is."

I thought, *Oh, good – finally*.

On Friday, Trudy and I drove to the Canada Border Services Agency. We arrived at the agency, gave our names to the receptionist and were ushered into the office of the head immigration officer. He told us to take a seat in front of his desk. We were all smiles until he began to speak. "Mr. McLaughlin, you have been in Canada illegally for the last two years."

I was shocked and objected strongly. I took out my work visa, which conveniently had his signature on it, and placed it on his desk. He looked at it and said, "You neglected to inform us of your DUI conviction, which we have recently noticed on your police records that you sent to the Consulate General of Canada with your application for landed immigrant status. He continued, "You should have told us when you came across the border in 1980. Had you told us, we would have denied your work visa."

I replied, "OK, sir, how can we correct this?"

His stern answer surprised us. "On Monday I want you to return here at 10:00 AM, prepared to return to the United States."

"What?" I exclaimed. He repeated his instructions and dismissed us. I pleaded with him, saying, "Sir, I was only eighteen years old when I was convicted of that crime thirteen years ago." I continued, "I am in full-time Christian work of the gospel. I don't know anyone on the west coast of the United States! Where do you expect me to go?"

He simply replied, "Anywhere in the USA!"

Then I asked him, "OK; well, how long will this take?"

"Monday 10:00 AM," was all he said, and the conversation was over.

We were confused and greatly disappointed as we drove back to Abbotsford. Once we got home we went straight to the CCC office and informed the director of our situation. We prayed together and he arranged for me to stay with a Campus Crusade supporter in Lynden, Washington, beginning on Monday, with the hope that it would only be for a few days.

Monday morning came and we drove to Lynden where I settled into a mobile trailer on a roofing company lot. Trudy and the children returned to Abbotsford. A couple of days later Trudy and I were driven to Seattle by one of Canada's Campus Crusade for Christ leaders for a meeting at the Consulate General of Canada. We had hoped that once the consul general heard our story, he would allow me to return to my home and ministry while waiting for Ottawa to clear this matter up. Unfortunately, that was not to be.

The meeting was brief and revealed that this could take more time than any of us preferred. There was a humorous moment when the consul general asked Trudy if she had a criminal record he should know about? Trudy looked at me, and then back at him and with a perfectly serious look she said, "Well, I did get stopped once for bald tires." To our surprise, he burst out in laughter – and we all joined in. It was the only lighthearted moment that day during our memorable meeting. The ride back was solemn. Our driver dropped me off in Lynden and then drove Trudy back to our house in Abbotsford. Trudy told me she would bring the children to visit on the weekend.

At this point, I became angry over the whole ordeal and boldly told the Lord just how I felt. Over the next few days, I made it a habit of visiting a small park where I would cry out to the Lord with all my frustrations. At times I would literally scream at Him. I would especially remind Him of the fact that my past sins were forgiven and that I felt He was being unfair since we had obediently come to Canada as He had clearly directed us to do. Looking back, I see how foolish I was in these daily discussions with God

Almighty, but He was gracious and listened to all my selfish and shameful complaints. Eventually He lovingly but firmly convicted me of my sin of anger. I repented in tears and asked Him what He wanted me to do?

The answer came through my US host. He recommended that I use this time in exile to find ways to minister. After more prayer and counsel from my host, I began preaching and sharing my testimony every chance I got. One highlight was preaching in the Light House Mission in Seattle. Everywhere I ministered, God blessed it, often with people repenting and receiving Christ. Little did I know at the time that the Lord was laying the groundwork for a future ministry in Washington state.

Once we realized this ordeal was going to take an exceptionally long time, we decided to fly back east to report to the area churches. We spent a few weeks meeting with supporters and ministering in the churches. God blessed this time as well. Following our time in New Hampshire we returned to the west coast. Trudy's mom came with us, and she had a wonderful time. We also took a break from everything, borrowed my host's camper, and drove down the Washington-Oregon coast for a week. It was a special time and we really needed it.

Eventually, I was allowed back into Canada and our entire family was given their landed immigration status papers. The exile took a full five months, but we gained many new friends and supporters during that time, most of whom have remained supporters to this very day.

As a result of the exile and the response to my preaching during that time, it became evident to us that God might be preparing me for an evangelistic preaching ministry. Consequently, we were encouraged by friends, and some pastors as well, to pursue a four-year Bible college degree. The consensus was that it would give me credibility with pastors and church leaders in the future.

BOB MCLAUGHLIN

After praying and seeking counsel, we approached our supervisors with our thoughts. At first it was frowned upon. In fact, one person told me in a meeting regarding our possible plans, "Bob, you are not capable of obtaining a degree. You are just not wired to study, especially for four years, and carry on a ministry at the same time. I recommend you reconsider and continue to serve the Lord in your current position."

Frankly, I was disappointed that she believed I was incapable of obtaining a college degree. In fact, this made me even more determined to get the education. I enjoy being told I cannot do something, especially when God has called me to do it! Eventually I received permission to attend college with the understanding that I was to carry on with my ministry while studying. I also had a verbal agreement with the leadership that if, while I was attending Bible college, I believed God was leading me away from my current ministry, it would be OK.

We made the move to the Bible college campus in August 1983. Thankfully, we were able to come to an agreement with the registrar to allow me to study and carry on an active ministry at the same time. I was given permission to hand in all my assignments past their due date and was able to miss a reasonable number of classes each semester. The hard-and-fast rule was that I had to be present for the exams.

I performed many ministry duties while attending college. I spearheaded a new campus ministry at the University of Regina and recruited students from the Bible college to join with me each week in that ministry. I recruited a busload of students to attend *KC 83,* a huge conference of over 17,000 students from all over North America, held in Kansas City, MO, where Dr. Billy Graham was a keynote speaker. I was involved in the advance set-up for the *Jesus Film* ministry in Brazil in 1984 and 1985. I recruited students for a Christmas break ministry in Mexico in 1985 and I also took a student with me to Guatemala City as part of the worldwide *Explo*

88

IN THE WAR

'86. All this made studies difficult but eventually I proved I could successfully do both school and ministry.

Then, a special invitation in 1986 brought about a major change to my ministry and our lives.

Chapter 14

AMSTERDAM '86 AND A NEW ORGANIZATION

By 1986, we were still studying at Bible college and serving in ministry. I had also been conducting several evangelistic meetings in small towns across the prairies; invitations to preach were becoming more frequent.

There were some humorous situations in those early days. One such incident occurred that winter when I was to hold a three-day campaign at a small church on the Canadian prairies. The community was a typical small, rural, prairie town. Several of my friends from Bible college came along with me to give their testimonies during the campaign, and we were billeted together in the home of a large Christian family.

I have always tried to practice my messages prior to preaching them to an audience but practicing in the homes where I was billeted was not possible. The thought of people being able to hear me rehearsing my message was a big distraction to me. So, I would often drive to a remote location, park my vehicle on a long stretch of road (in a perfect spot where I was able to see cars approaching both from the rear as well as the front), and then proceed to practice my message.

As an evangelistic preacher, I seldom remained stationary during my message. Even when rehearsing the sermon in my vehicle, my

BOB MCLAUGHLIN

arms would flail, and I would often pound the steering wheel for emphasis. Of course, when a vehicle approached, I would stop my flailing and pretend to be just sitting perfectly still, reading a map.

After about thirty minutes of rehearsing my message for the upcoming service that night, I noticed a vehicle coming towards me, so I quit rehearsing and just sat still, waiting for the car to pass by. However, this car seemed to be slowing down as it approached me, and then it stopped right beside my car. I looked at the man as he opened his window and noticed that he seemed quite upset. I opened my window and he shouted, "Are you OK?"

I replied, "Yes, thank you, I am fine."

To which he shouted, "Well, we don't think so!" and rolled up his window and sped away. I thought that it was kind of weird. Why would he say 'we' when he was the only one in his car, and had he seen me? But, how was that possible? Within a few moments I saw him speeding by, going back to wherever he came from. *What a strange man*, I thought.

I finished rehearsing and drove back to the farm to get ready for the evening service. When I entered the house, my host approached me and asked if anyone had bothered me while I was out. I told him about the encounter with the man on the road. My host began to laugh and said, "Bob, that fellow is a farmer who lives down the road from where you were parked. He called us a few minutes ago and said there was a guy out on the highway bouncing around in his car. I asked him what kind of a car he was referring to and he described your car to a T. The fellow said he and his family took turns watching you from their home with high-powered binoculars. At that point, my host told his neighbor that the guy they saw through their binoculars was an evangelist who was conducting a three-day crusade at their church and invited them to come hear me preach. The farmer on the other end of the phone simply grunted and promptly hung up.

92

IN THE WAR

This crusade was a great success, and many were saved during those three days. At the end of the crusade, we all had a good laugh over the family who witnessed me rehearsing my message through their binoculars. I'm sure I was a sight to behold. Unfortunately, they never came to the crusade, but I did decide that it would be wise to find a different place to rehearse my messages.

From 1985 through early summer 1986, we were preparing for my first major crusade to be held in upstate Washington – in a beautiful Dutch Reformed farming community. This came about as a direct result of the many contacts I had made while I was in exile in 1983, waiting for the Canadian government to grant us our landed immigrant status. This was a major crusade for me because it involved more than one church. Several churches had agreed to work together to conduct a four-day crusade from August 7-10, 1986.

Before this crusade happened, I was privileged to receive an invitation from the Billy Graham Evangelistic Association to attend a huge conference for itinerant evangelists, – *Amsterdam 86,* which took place in Amsterdam, The Netherlands in July 1986. This conference was significant in that it changed the course we were currently on. It was during the conference that the Lord clearly called me to do the work of an itinerant preaching evangelist. I remember the moment God confirmed this specific calling. It was during one of Dr. Graham's messages when he thrust his hand out over the podium, pointed his finger (it seemed like he was pointing right at me as I sat in the midst of 10,000 evangelists from all over the world) and said, "You are here because God has called you to do the work of an itinerant evangelist."

That was it; it was confirmed! This was my calling, and I must obey. Jesus said to *"Go into all the world and preach the gospel to all creation."* (Mark 16:15 NASB) This would be my future.

Even before Dr. Graham's message was over, God gave me an idea – perhaps a vision. I thought that we could possibly remain on staff with Campus Crusade and conduct large evangelistic campaigns

93

BOB MCLAUGHLIN

across North America and around the globe, utilizing the help of thousands of CCC staff. At that time, evangelistic campaigns of this type still appealed to area churches and were seen as beneficial for church growth. My thought was that we could use CCC staff, already positioned around the world, to be responsible for the advance training and follow-up necessary for such campaigns.

I knew Dr. Bill Bright was also attending this historic conference, so I prayed that the Lord would arrange for me to meet with him and share my thoughts. The Lord answered my request almost immediately. Upon the close of that plenary session, everyone began making their way from the huge conference center for a break time. I was pleased when I spotted Dr. Bright walking alone to his hotel. I thanked the Lord that I met up with him, then came up alongside of him and introduced myself. "I remember you," Dr. Bright said. "As I recall, you are serving with us in Canada."

"Yes, sir we are," I said, and then I continued, "May I share with you what I believe God is currently doing in my life?"

"Yes, of course, please do," was his reply."

"Dr. Bright," I said, "I believe with all my heart that I am called to be an itinerant evangelist, and that's why I have been invited to this conference, and today, Dr. Graham's message confirmed my calling." I continued to share my thoughts with him. "There is a desperate need to get the gospel out today. Is it possible that Campus Crusade could combine efforts with churches in reaching the world for Christ, by providing this type of mass evangelistic campaign in cities all over the world? Churches are still willing to work together like this and God has blessed CCC with thousands of dedicated staff members who could help them to reap a harvest for Christ in their cities. Not only could we provide the evangelist, but also our staff could help with the preparations for such an event and provide the necessary training for counseling and follow-up afterwards. What do you think Dr. Bright?"

He replied, "Bob, I love your enthusiasm and I love your vision. There is a pilot project happening right now in New York City with

IN THE WAR

one of our staff, who has the intent of doing exactly what you are proposing. I really like what you are thinking, however we must consult with your Canadian leadership about this possibility." He continued, "I will be in Victoria, BC for the Canadian staff conference in a few days. I will arrange a meeting for us together with your wife and the director. Meanwhile, let's be in prayer about this proposal." I thanked him for his time, and we agreed to meet in Canada.

The Canadian staff conference took place a couple of weeks later at the University of Victoria, on beautiful Vancouver Island. As promised, Dr. Bright arranged a meeting in his hotel room with us and the Canadian director. Dr. Bright opened our meeting in prayer and then asked us to share our vision with our director. Once we finished, Dr. Bright asked the director two key questions. The first was, "Do you believe Bob is an evangelist?"

The director replied, "I think he is."

Next, Dr. Bright asked him, "Does Bob share his faith one on one with people?" Again, the answer was in the affirmative. Then the big question came from Dr. Bright. He asked, "What do you think? Can you envision Bob's vision?" The director's answer was a firm 'NO' and that he had plans for me to become the Here's Life provincial director of Saskatchewan.

As I processed what he said, two things came to my mind immediately. One, this was the first we had heard anything about even being offered that position, or for that matter, any position. Secondly, I knew that I was not called to that type of ministry.

Before anything else was said I responded, "Well, thank you for that offer, but to be perfectly honest with you, this is the first we have heard of this, and furthermore I am called by God to a ministry of itinerant evangelistic preaching."

At this point I knew that Dr. Bright was faced with a difficult situation. He seemed to lean towards agreeing with my vision, but as the leader of such a huge organization, he needed to trust his chain of command with this type of decision. Trudy and I have always had the utmost respect for the Campus Crusade founder, but it grew even more when he said the following, "Bob, I believe that you are an evangelist, and that the Lord has a perfect plan for you and Trudy." He continued, "If CCC is not capable of accommodating your vision, you have my blessing to pursue your vision with all your heart." Then he offered a beautiful prophetic prayer of blessing on our calling to preach the gospel to all creation.

Later that same day, during a break in the conference, we informed our leaders that we would be giving our official resignation in writing shortly after the conference.

We have always found it strangely interesting that, when God calls a person out of an existing ministry to begin or join another ministry, then that calling automatically comes into question. Many staff members strongly suggested that we were making a mistake to leave such a huge organization. One almost humorous comment was: "Bob, what are you going to do about financial support if you and Trudy leave our organization?"

I responded to this individual with, "Friend, we are not changing gods here, we are only changing ministries." Then I quoted the verse of Scripture, *"And* my God will supply all your needs according to His riches in *glory in Christ Jesus."* (Philippians 4:19 NASB) He stormed away.

A few days later, we officially resigned after eight wonderful years of ministry with CCC and soon began a new evangelistic ministry called Bob McLaughlin Evangelistic Association Inc. BMEA was governed by a board of directors and incorporated as a non-profit Christian organization. We began conducting many crusades across Canada, as well as some in the United States. Though these crusades were conducted in small towns, the response to the gospel was astounding. In some towns, as many as ten percent of the community publicly indicated that they wanted to receive Christ. The ministry's acceptance was on the rise.

As the 1980's ended and we entered the 1990's, I was receiving invitations to preach in some prominent churches across Canada, England, and Russia. Television appearances on Christian programs in Toronto, as well as televised services at a large Toronto church helped to boost awareness of my ministry. BMEA also began ministering on a wider international scale in India, the Philippines, and countries in Africa. These campaigns were held in cooperation with, and served under the umbrella of, other ministries which invited BMEA to assist them in evangelistic campaigns.

Also, a window of opportunity for evangelism opened from 1989 through 1997 when the Holy Spirit swept across the entire former Soviet Union with unprecedented waves of spiritual power. As a result, the country was open to BMEA to conduct campaigns from 1990 through 1997 in cooperation with the Russian Union of Evangelical Christians-Baptists. BMEA was just one of many North American Christian organizations involved in this amazing move of God, and these campaigns in the former Soviet Union were nothing short of miraculous

Bob meets Billy Graham

Canadian Crusade

Canadian Crusade

PART FOUR
MINISTRY EXPANDS

Chapter 15

THE BEGINNING OF THE END

I cannot express the feelings of gratitude to God that nearly overwhelmed me as I climbed the steps to the pulpit. The date was November 4, 1990. I was an evangelist with a message of hope. I gazed out at the packed congregation in amazement. The people occupied not only every seat in the lower sanctuary and the balcony, including the stairwells, but every available spot in the aisles as well. These were people hungry for God and I was more than honored to be the vessel God had chosen to feed them His Word. I remember thinking how unbelievable it was that I was about to preach in the most famous Baptist church in all of Russia. However, it was true, and I was ready to bring the gospel to the people of the First Baptist Church of Moscow. But before I would begin to preach, something would happen that was to bring about the beginning of the end.

The very fact that I was in Russia was nothing short of a miracle itself. A few weeks prior, I was sitting at the rear of another congregation in a very large auditorium on the prairies of Saskatchewan. The preacher was a man who had recently returned from Russia. I was captivated by the stories he shared about the hunger for God of the Russian people. I remember thinking how awesome it would be to travel to a land where the people not only eagerly listened

BOB MCLAUGHLIN

to the Word of God, but also, with genuine tears of repentance, would stream forward to seek God's forgiveness of their sins. How foreign this seemed to us in North America, but it was true. There was a window of opportunity open in the land of Russia. God had answered the prayers of His people and brought down the Iron Curtain, to the surprise of us all, I might add. It all happened so quickly and unexpectedly that most of North America was caught by surprise. Though we prayed fervently, truth be known, that was one prayer most of us doubted the Lord would answer in our time.

Before his sermon was done I leaned over to Trudy and said, "What am I doing running around North America and beating my head against the wall looking for opportunities to preach to people who don't want to listen, when I could board a plane right now and fly to Russia where the people not only want to hear the message, but want to repent and experience His love and forgiveness?"

Trudy, as always, responded with words of wisdom, "Well, let's pray about it."

We went home that afternoon, and we did pray about it, as Trudy had suggested. I continued in prayer for the remainder of the day, sensing that God was indeed about to do something. A burning desire to go to Russia was heavy on my heart throughout the night. I prayed that if God was leading me to Russia that He would give confirmation. I asked Him to confirm it in several ways.

First, I felt it was of utmost importance that He gives me confirmation through His Word, the Bible. It came right away. I picked up my Bible and it fell open to Genesis 42. I read the first two verses, *"Now Jacob saw that there was grain in Egypt, and Jacob said to his sons, 'Why are you staring at one another?' He said, 'Behold, I have heard that there is grain in Egypt; go down there and buy some* for us from that place, so that we may live and not die.'" (NASB) There it was – my confirmation from God. He was saying to me through this passage, "Your invitations for ministry in North America have dried up, but I have opened a window for you in Russia. Don't just

102

IN THE WAR

stand there! Go where the grain (the harvest) is available in plenty."
I eagerly shared this with Trudy, who agreed with me that this was
God's confirmation for me through His Word.

Secondly, I asked Him for confirmation through one of His children. Unsolicited, I needed for some child of God to say that this
was of God. And thirdly, I asked for confirmation with the cash
needed for such a mission. Well, the next morning the telephone
rang. I answered the phone and found myself talking to an elderly
brother in the Lord. Burt was a man with a burdened heart for the
'lost' of the world and had been a prayer partner in our evangelistic
ministry. What he said to me that morning shocked me, and at the
same time excited me, as my spirit quickened within me. He said,
"Bob, what's going on in your life right now? I was unable to sleep
last night. The Lord laid you and your ministry on my heart, and I
have been in prayer most of the night for you. So, I thought maybe
you could shed some light on why God guided me to do that." I
knew this was God's doing so I shared with him. I told him about
the sermon I had heard the day before, that I had been praying
about the possibility that God was leading me to go to the Soviet
Union to preach the gospel, and that I was seeking His confirmation.
Burt was silent for a few moments and then he said, "Don't hesi-
tate, and make all the necessary plans to go to Russia! God has told
me just now to pay for your flights." Wow! God had answered my
prayers and given me the last two confirmations that I had asked
for. I knew at that moment that I was going to Russia.

There was a lot to do over the next few days, so I wasted no
time in taking care of the necessary preparations. I had a good
contact in London, England. I had first met Klaus a year or two
before when I preached at his home church in Richmond, a suburb
of London. The Duke Street Baptist Church was a prominent and
highly respected church. I phoned Klaus and told him of my plans.
He told me he might be able to help me in obtaining some Russian

103

contacts. We agreed that I should plan to spend several days in London prior to going on to Russia.

It turned out that my London contact had some friends who had just returned from Russia, so he arranged for a meeting at his home. During this meeting his friends briefly shared their experiences in Russia, in an attempt to prepare me for my upcoming time there. They were able to give me the names of three Russian contacts, which I carefully wrote down, as well as where I could expect to find them once I arrived. The meeting ended with all of us praying for the Lord's anointing and blessing upon my time in Russia.

A day or two later, I boarded my flight from London Heathrow Airport to Moscow. To say the least, I was more than excited and full of anticipation. My adrenalin was coursing through my body as I reflected on my childhood fears during the very intense 'cold war' between the Soviet Union and the United States. I had vivid memories of watching Nikita Khrushchev on TV, slamming and pounding his shoe on his desk during a United Nations assembly and shouting, "We will bury America!!" Those words seemed to be ringing in my ears.

My memories intensified as my flight got closer to Russia. One such memory was of our elementary class, during the early 1960's, rehearsing emergency atomic bomb attack drills. When the alarm rang, teachers in each classroom would shout instructions for every student to crawl under their desks and cover their heads with their hands. Now as an adult, I think to myself: *How absurd that we were led to believe that this almost silly action could somehow protect us from an atomic bomb dropped by Russian planes.*

Another vivid memory was of me, as a young boy, lying on my top bunk, unable to sleep. I would gaze out my window and look intently into the night sky for parachuting Russian soldiers coming to kill us all. These were frightening concerns for a little boy.

Before long, my disturbing memories were abruptly inter-rupted when our captain announced our descent into Moscow. I

IN THE WAR

pushed my memories deep down inside of me as I deplaned and entered the airport. I cleared customs and immigration without difficulty. Once I gathered all my belongings, I was approached by a Russian official holding a placard with my name on it. The individual was connected to the Russian organization called Intourist, which dealt strictly with US and international individuals entering Russia in those days. I was immediately escorted to a waiting car and driven to an Intourist hotel in downtown Moscow. All Intourist hotels were closely watched, and the people staying there were constantly under surveillance. These preselected hotels, by Intourist, allowed the Russian government authorities – the KGB, to keep close tabs on all the guests' activities.

Over the years of ministry that followed, I was closely watched by the Russian KGB. I remember at times that it was almost humorous as I came to easily recognize these 'servants' of the government. I would see them sitting in their Russian Lada automobiles just outside my hotel, smoking their cigarettes, reading their newspapers and even wearing sunglasses. Each morning as I would leave the hotel for my jog I would often shout in my best Russian, "Dobroye utro!!" (English translation: "Good morning") They would never reply, but just stare at me and watch me jog off. I would also spot them in many of my early evangelistic campaigns held in the various Houses of Culture.

I'm getting ahead of myself, so back to my first visit to Russia. After arriving at the Moscow airport, the Intourist official who was waiting for me, escorted me to the Moscow Hotel and helped me to get checked in. I was then escorted to my room and given some guidelines. Eventually I was left to myself in a small room which was sparsely fitted with furniture. I was also aware that the room would be 'bugged' by the government, but at least it was clean and warm. I was tired after my long journey, so I took a wake-up shower before going down for supper. The hotel restaurant was an interesting experience. I managed to have a waiter who spoke good broken English, so I was able to order a meal. I quickly caught on that the service would be faster and better if I said I was paying in US dollars. In fact, every financial exchange was prefaced with the common question, "Are you paying in rubles or US dollars?"

Knowing that the following day was a Sunday, I was excited and determined that I would order a car in the morning to take me to the First Baptist Church of Moscow. Following a nearly sleepless night (I guess I was just excited), I took the elevator down and approached the front desk. The lady behind the desk, who was a bit gruff but somewhat cordial, asked in English just what it was I wanted. I told her I needed a car and driver to go to the First Baptist Church. She said I would need to pay the driver in US dollars rather than Russian rubles. Once I assured her, I could do that, she instructed me to go back to my room and she would call me when she had arranged the car and driver. A few minutes later I got the call saying my car and driver were waiting, so I quickly went down to the lobby. She instructed my hired driver to take me to the First Baptist Church. Upon my arrival, I paid him in US dollars and entered the church.

I was still excited, to say the least. However, my excitement was quickly interrupted as I was being received into the church by the saints with a holy kiss. I was truly overwhelmed with the whole reception. To my utter astonishment, one by one, men dressed in black suits with black ties grabbed me and hugged me tightly (too close for my comfort, I might add) and then proceeded to greet me, as all Christian Russian men did in those days, by placing their lips smack on my lips with a Christian holy kiss. I was in absolute shock, not to mention being slightly nauseated with each man's greeting!! Only by the grace of God was I able to accept these greetings of love in Christ and they were indeed true greetings of Christian love.

I was quickly noticed as an American visitor, so I was escorted to the senior pastor's small office where, upon entering, this man of God stood and greeted me in the same manner as the others

IN THE WAR

had. Following the greeting, he introduced himself as the Reverend Alexei Bichkov. I later discovered that he was general secretary of the Soviet Baptist Church, and that he had been very influential in gaining the government's approval to invite the Rev. Billy Graham to Russia back in May of 1982, for the *World Conference of Religious Workers for Saving the Sacred Gift of Life from Nuclear Catastrophe*. In other words, he was a very prominent Christian leader in Russia.

He asked me why I was in Russia, so I shared with him the whole story leading up to my being in his office. To my great surprise, he took out his pen and handwrote a lengthy letter of endorsement in English for me to share with pastors back in Canada and America. He also wrote one for Russian leaders. I was overwhelmed with this dear man's generosity. I guess he saw the future potential of it all.

After our initial meeting, Rev. Alexei took me downstairs for lunch. He seated me beside a man whose very presence would totally confirm to me that this whole event, of my being in Russia, was nothing short of the work of God. Once I was settled into my chair, I turned to introduce myself to this fellow next to me. I discovered that not only did he speak English, but he was the very man of God who was used by the Lord to influence me to come to Russia, when Trudy and I heard him preach back in Saskatchewan two months earlier. Clearly, this was indeed God's doing. Together we rejoiced over how the Lord had worked in both our lives. Before he left me, he gave me a few helpful tips for my time in the Soviet Union.

After lunch, Rev. Alexei invited me to preach in the second service, so I asked him when that would be and he replied, "Right now." I was thrilled and honored. He informed me that the people needed to hear the message God had for them, through me. The church was packed, but as I mentioned earlier in this chapter, the beginning of the end was upon me.

I sat beside Rev. Alexei, who would be my interpreter. As the service began, I realized they were going to serve communion. Unknown to me, they serve communion in every service. It's a

107

beautiful ceremony and most honoring to the Lord. The deacons served the communion wine with large silver goblets and they each had a white towel which they used to wipe the goblet clean after serving the wine to each parishioner. As I watched this beautiful ceremony unfold before my eyes, I wondered if they were serving real wine. At this point I leaned over to Alexei and asked if the large goblets contained actual wine. Alexei said with a smile, "Of course Bob, the Bible says wine not Welch's!" I chuckled a bit, and began to anticipate the situation I now found myself in.

A raging battle began to take place in my heart and mind: *Should I partake and consume the wine or simply abstain?* I had not had a drink of alcohol for seventeen and a half years. I began to reason that God must have totally delivered me from alcoholism and that He was the one Who had placed me in front of these dear people, hungry for the Word of God. I continued reasoning with the Lord that if I were to bypass the cup, that action could make a silent statement that I was abstaining because of an unconfessed sin in my life. I reasoned that, in not drinking the communion wine, I would automatically lose credibility with the congregation. I was keenly aware that all eyes were staring at me, or at least it seemed that way.

Then I challenged God by reminding Him of a verse of Scripture, *"Therefore if anyone is in Christ, he is* a new creature; the old things passed away; behold, new things have come." (2 Corinthians 5:17 NASB) I now admit that I was just cocky, arrogant and foolish to challenge God with this. I knew I should avoid taking the wine. The truth is I was really anticipating the taste of that wine entering my mouth. Furthermore, to my great shame, I openly admit that I was not thinking of the blood of Christ when I took of the wine. No, sadly, I was thinking what all classic alcoholics think, that now I can socially drink again. This event, unknown to me, was the beginning of the end.

IN THE WAR

Duke Street Baptist Church London England

Bob with Rev Steven Olford

Bob with Dr. Leighton Ford

Bob with Dr. John W. White

Chapter 16

A REFLECTION OF JONAH IN LENINGRAD

The service on November 4, 1990, in the First Baptist Church of Moscow, was truly blessed of God. Following communion, Rev. Alexei introduced me as the visiting speaker. My texts were John 3:14-16 and Numbers 21:4-9, with emphasis on the evening encounter that Nicodemus had with Jesus and His reference to Moses and the bronze serpent. The moment I opened my mouth to read Scripture, I sensed an anointing and power from the Holy Spirit. I preached a simple evangelistic message with unusual authority. I was honored that Rev. Alexei was my interpreter. When I gave the invitation to repent and receive Christ as Lord and Savior, many in the congregation made their way through the crowded church to get to the front. Rev. Alexei closed the service in prayer and dismissed the congregation. Follow-up was done by members of the congregation, so Pastor Alexei then escorted me to his office and we thanked God for His obvious blessing on the service. We embraced, and I left the church, rejoicing, as I returned to my hotel.

The following day was a full free day to spend in Moscow, so I made plans to tour the city. What does one do when in Moscow

BOB MCLAUGHLIN

for a day? The obvious! So, I took a taxi to the famous [2]Red Square tourist attraction. I was surprised to see the entire square crowded with Russian soldiers. My curiosity was aroused, and I began to inquire why there were so many soldiers. Eventually, I found a young couple, Serge and Nadia, who spoke good English. They informed me that it was nearing the time of year for the annual Bolshevik Revolution parade. I had forgotten that I would be in Russia during this important national event. As I walked around the square with this couple, I decided to ask Serge if he would interpret for me so I could greet the soldiers. Some of the soldiers spoke good English and greeted me back with huge smiles on their faces. They looked very military-like in their uniforms. I said I was an American and asked if we could be friends. One very big soldier gave me a bear hug, and hoisted me up as he said, in broken English, "Da sure, we you good friend". He continued hugging me until I thought I was doomed because I could barely breathe. He eventually let me down to the roar of laughter coming from the soldiers. I asked if I could have a photo with them and they readily agreed. It was a fun moment and one that I shall always remember.

We also toured [3]Lenin's tomb, where we were instructed to remain in single file and move slowly through the tomb. Talking was strictly forbidden as we walked along and this was controlled by armed guards, both inside as well as outside of the tomb. I remember praying and thanking God that Lenin was no longer alive to inflict his evil beliefs and actions on the people of Russia, but that did remind me that he was most likely in hell.

As we continued our tour of the area, Serge and Nadia took me through the renowned [4]GUM Department Store, which faces

---

[2] *Red Square is the city square in the heart of Moscow.*

[3] *Vladimir Lenin was instrumental in having tens of thousands killed or interned in concentration camps in his attempt to further his socialistic ideals.*

[4] *The GUM Department Store is Russia's State department store.*

IN THE WAR

Red Square. We finished our day at the famous new [5]McDonald's Restaurant, where I bought my guides a 'thank you' dinner. McDonald's opened on January 30, 1990, – ten months before this – and still there were huge line-ups. As I recall, we stood in line for nearly an hour just to get in. However, the food was excellent, and I was impressed!

Later that evening, I was to take an overnight train to the city of Minsk in Belarus. On this, my first trip to the USSR, Intourist had arranged for all my in-country travel from city to city to be by overnight trains. It would be my first train ride in the former Soviet Union, and I was in for a big surprise.

I discovered that the train system in the USSR was a reliable and punctual travel system. Almost all of the trains were the same in style and layout. There was a long hallway on one side of each car with curtained windows, and a railing – the length of the train car – attached to the wall. The small compartments, off of the hallway, contained four bunk beds, two on each side. Between the bunks and next to the window was a tiny table. I made my way to my compartment, opened the door, and entered the room. I was honestly relieved to see that I was alone in the compartment.

However, that quickly changed when two women and a man entered the compartment. They greeted me in Russian with smiles on their faces. I assume my discomfort showed, as I was not smiling. Since I could not speak Russian, I began making hand motions, attempting to say that they must be in the wrong compartment – after all, I was a man, and so women should not be in the same compartment, especially since it was an overnight sleeping train. They simply smiled and said something back in Russian. They showed me their tickets and sure enough, they were in the right compartment. I was horrified and felt deceived. No one had informed me

---

[5] Moscow's McDonald's restaurant was the largest one in the world at the time.

BOB MCLAUGHLIN

that this was a common practice, in much of Europe and in the USSR, when travelling by train.

As the train began moving down the rails, I sat on my bunk, near the table, and tried to figure out what I should do next. The car attendant came to our compartment to serve hot tea, or as the Russians would say, "chay." After tea, and more hand motions in a desperate, but unsuccessful, attempt to convince them to leave, I decided to check out the other compartments. Towards the back of the car, next to the toilet, I found an empty compartment and I quickly moved all my belongings. I stayed up until the train began slowing down as it was approaching a stop. It was late in the evening as people boarded the train, so I crawled into the bottom bunk, turned off the compartment lights and pretended I was sleeping. There was some Russian chatter back and forth and a bit of commotion as a group considered entering my compartment. I heard the word, "American," in the conversation and I was sure that they were cursing me. Apparently, the attendant told the people to go to another compartment and leave the dumb American alone. This strategy seemed to work for the entire trip. I was relieved, to say the least.

I arrived in Minsk the next morning having slept very little for fear that I would be removed from the bunk that I stole from someone the night before. Also, the very strong smell of train engine fuel permeated the compartments all night long. Upon exiting the train, I was approached by another Intourist staff member bearing a placard with my name on it. He escorted me to an Intourist car and I was whisked away to my hotel. My time in Minsk was good. I met with a few pastors, and tentative plans for ministry were developed.

On the night of November 7, I took another adventurous overnight train trip, this time to Kiev. Things were becoming somewhat routine for me and I knew what to expect once I arrived in the Ukrainian city. Sure enough, there was a man from Intourist holding a placard with my name

IN THE WAR

on it. He helped me gather my belongings and off we went to the hotel, selected in advance by the government, for my stay in Kiev.

I settled into my room. An hour later, I was drawn to the window to take in an amazing, and I might add, historic event. I was thankful my room was facing the main street because right outside my window, and several floors down, the annual October Revolution Day Parade was in full swing. Just like when I was a kid, I was fascinated with the amazing display of military might. I took picture after picture and enjoyed the best possible view right from my hotel window. The military armament and the number of marching soldiers were impressive. However, I was somewhat taken aback to see that very few Soviet people were on the sidelines. I knew that in all the televised parades that I had seen in years past, masses of people were forced to line the streets, in order to show their approval and pride of the amazing military might on display. But, we were now in a different time in history, and "perestroika" (restructuring) was in full bloom.

In March of 1985, the General Secretary of the Communist Party of the Soviet Union, Mikhail S. Gorbachev, began to introduce his historic dual program of "perestroika" and "glasnost" (openness) for the entire Soviet Union, sending the nation down a fast and new dramatic course of life. History has demonstrated that this new program made amazing and profound changes in the Soviet economy and, more importantly, their international relationships. Over the next few years these actions would bring about the collapse of the Soviet Union in 1991, and an end to the Cold War.

While in Kiev, I was able to meet with another pastor who was on my list of contacts. Now that I had successfully met with him, I continued on my way to the city of Leningrad (now known as St. Petersburg). This would be my last stop before returning to Moscow and catching my flight home. I was looking forward to my time in Leningrad. I knew that this city was even more beautiful than the other cities that I had visited on this trip. Upon arrival, I was again taken to the hotel that was arranged by Intourist, and I checked into my room. I then began to argue with myself

115

BOB MCLAUGHLIN

about whether or not I should attempt to contact the last name on my list, a pastor living in Leningrad. To my great shame I chose to disobey God.

I knew what God wanted me to do, but at this point I became like Jonah. I reasoned with myself that this was an historic city and I deserved to become a tourist for one day. After all, I had been successful in making contacts for future ministry in all of the other cities. I freshened up and deliberately stuffed the piece of paper, with the name of my contacts, deep into my shirt pocket. Of the three names on the list, only one remained unchecked. I pushed a slight feeling of guilt aside and proceeded to become a tourist. I went to the front desk and promptly ordered an English-speaking driver and a car to take me on my tour of beautiful Leningrad.

A few minutes later my car and driver arrived and took me for an all-day sightseeing trip. We toured the [6]Winter Palace, the [7]Palace Square, the [8]Alexander Column, the [9]Palace Bridge, [10]Nevsky Prospekt, the [11]Anichkov Bridge, the [12]Cathedral of Saints Peter and Paul, the [13]Bronze Horseman, and the famous Russian Cruiser, [14]Aurora. The Aurora battleship had been moored in Leningrad and was preserved as a museum ship for tourists. She is known for many historic events, but the one

---

[6] *The Winter Palace was the official residence of the Russian Emperors from 1732 to 1917.*

[7] *The Palace Square is the big open space in front of the Winter Palace that connects the Palace Bridge and Nevsky Prospekt.*

[8] *The Alexander Column is the focal point of the Palace Square.*

[9] *The Palace Bridge spans the Neva River by the Palace Square.*

[10] *Nevsky Prospekt is the main street of Leningrad.*

[11] *The Anichkov Bridge is a very old and famous bridge which spans the Fontanka River.*

[12] *The Cathedral of Saints Peter and Paul is a Russian Orthodox cathedral built by Peter the Great on Hare Island, in the Neva River.*

[13] *The Bronze Horseman is an equestrian statue of Peter the Great.*

[14] *The Aurora was a Cruiser which was assigned to Russia's Baltic Fleet during World War 1 and World War 11.*

IN THE WAR

most people remember is the incident which took place on the night of October 25, 1917, at 9:40 PM. A blank shot fired from her forecastle gun signaled the start of an assault on the Winter Palace, which brought on the [15]October Revolution.

After touring the city for a full day, I was exhausted and hungry, so I instructed my driver to take me back to my hotel. My plan was to have supper and then go straight to bed. But God had other plans for this disobedient evangelist.

On entering the hotel, I went straight to the restaurant with the anticipation of having a nice meal before retiring for the evening. I was disappointed to discover that the hotel restaurant was not open, and it seemed rather odd to me that it would be closed during dinner time. Disheartened, I took the elevator to my floor, having accepted the possibility that I could go to bed without any supper. The elevator doors opened, and I began walking down the hall towards my room. As I walked along, I noticed a colorful glass door, partially opened, on my left. I saw that the room had been converted into a small kiosk where they served sandwiches, coffee and soda pop. I thanked the Lord and entered the room. There were only four little tables and one man sat alone, drinking his coffee. I noticed that there were only a few sandwiches and one or two Pepsi Colas behind the glass display. I purchased a sandwich and a Pepsi and then I sat down to enjoy the sparse meal while looking forward to a good night's sleep.

As I sat in that small room, I could feel an overwhelming sensation that someone was staring at me. I looked up and saw that the only man in the room was the same fellow whom I had noticed earlier. He was literally grinning from ear to ear as he sat facing me and looking intently at me. This struck me as very odd, and frankly made me feel very uncomfortable. Then a thought hit me, *oh my, I think he's gay!* This made me eat faster and want to run to my room. I am not homophobic, but I do detest being hit on by gay people.

---

[15] *The October Revolution, also known as the Bolshevik Revolution, was a revolt under Lenin which moved Russia to Communism.*

Before I could take my last bite, he was standing beside my table, wearing the same grin. As I gingerly looked up at his face, I noticed that he had blond hair, a round face, and pleasant yet piercing eyes. My flesh began to crawl and before I could attempt to say a word, he blurted out, "Why are you here?" I sat and stared at him in absolute disbelief. He simply repeated his question. "Why are you here?" His English was good, but he had an accent I did not recognize – it clearly was not Russian.

I asked, "Who are you?"

He replied, "That's not important!" Before I could respond to his answer he continued, "What's important here is that you tell me who you are and why you are here?" Before I could answer he startled me with the following statement, "Listen, I have been sent here by God to meet you. I have been waiting here for four hours for you. When you walked in, I knew you were the one I had been waiting for. You are an evangelist, are you not?" At this point, I wondered if I was dreaming. Was this happening? It was all surreal and frankly bizarre. He asked me again, "Are you an evangelist?" I finally gave in and confessed that I was indeed an evangelist. At that point he said, "OK, let's go to your room. I have every possible contact you need."

I said to him, "I don't know you and you are asking to go with me to my room? You can't possibly be serious!"

He said, "Yes, I am very serious; let's go." In absolute disbelief, I got up and led this total stranger to my hotel room. We entered the room together; he immediately headed for the telephone, sat down and made a phone call. He spoke to someone in Russian, and then wrote down a name and number on a piece of paper. He stood, handed me the paper and said, "Tomorrow you have a lunch appointment with this man, here at the hotel." I was still in shock when he concluded with, "My work here is done. Make sure you meet this man tomorrow. Goodbye." He opened the door, smiled at me and left my room.

I looked at the name and number on the paper and I couldn't believe what I saw. My heart wrenched as I realized whose name was written there. My hand shook as I took out the paper that I had earlier

IN THE WAR

disobediently pushed down into my shirt pocket. It was the name and number of my third contact.

I fell to my knees, then stretched prostrate on the floor and wept bitter tears of repentance. I confessed my sin over and over for the next hour or so. I was ashamed of myself and felt totally unworthy to even be here. As I gathered my wits and pulled myself up off the floor, I began to wonder just who this man was that God had sent to meet me. Could it simply be an obedient Christian who was led to my hotel by God Himself? Or was he an angel sent by God to confront this disobedient evangelist with his blatant sin? You can decide for yourself, but as for me, I know beyond a shadow of doubt that he was an angel sent by God.

I had become like Jonah. He knew exactly what he was supposed to do, but by an act of his will, he deliberately chose to disobey God. I was guilty of the very same sin.

When Jonah finally obeyed God, an entire city repented, and God spared the people of Nineveh. It turned out that over the next seven years, this Leningrad contact would be used by God to open up all of Russia for me. Just like Jonah, I too had to repent and obey God, so that He could work in the lives of the Russian people.

Lenin's Tomb in Red Square

Soldiers in Red Square

IN THE WAR

The Aurora Ship

Rev. Peter Konavolchik

Chapter 17

YOU ARE CROCODILE MEAT

I had taken this trip numerous times in the past. The long, tiring flight began in Regina, Saskatchewan where once again, Trudy and the children dropped me off at the airport. I kissed them goodbye, and we began yet another three-week separation.

I checked in and before long I was on my way to Minneapolis, Minnesota on a Northwest Airlines commuter flight. When I arrived in Minneapolis, I went through US customs and quickly made my way to the Northwest frequent flyer lounge, to await my transatlantic flight to Amsterdam, the Netherlands.

The night flight to Amsterdam was smooth and uneventful. Once we landed at Schiphol airport, I again made my way to the frequent flyer lounge. Several hours later I boarded the beautiful KLM 747 for my long flight to Africa. As was often the case, I was upgraded to business class in the upper deck. Though it was clearly more comfortable in business class, it was still a long and tiring flight to Lilongwe, in the country of Malawi, which is known as 'the warm heart of Africa.' I had always been fascinated with the continent of Africa, and I was excited to preach the gospel once again to the people of Malawi.

In previous years, we had conducted several campaigns in both Africa and Asia in conjunction with other evangelistic organizations.

BOB MCLAUGHLIN

This was one of those campaigns where I would have the privilege of serving under the umbrella of another ministry.

As the huge 747 descended closer and closer to our landing in Lilongwe, I drank in the beauty of the countryside, through my window. I could see the remote villages scattered across the vast, hot, dry land, which was interconnected by pencil line dirt paths crisscrossing the landscape. The thrill of touching down again on the African continent returned afresh and washed over me. Yes, there was something almost magical about being in Africa.

The blast of hot air hit me as I descended the stairs from the aircraft and made my way across the tarmac to enter the airport terminal. Once I cleared Malawian customs and collected my luggage, I was met by my national team members who drove me to the Baptist guest house in the city. The guest house, which was to be my home for the duration of the campaign, was clean, well-kept, and comfortable for African standards.

I learned a long time ago that no two campaigns are ever the same. In fact, truthfully, no two evangelistic meetings are ever the same. This campaign would prove to be unique.

Each morning, I would rise early and go jogging before breakfast. Later, the team would come for me and we would head out to the first of several places, where we would minister that day. Getting to some of these villages, which were out in the bush, often proved to be a challenge. Almost daily, we encountered extremely rutted and dusty dirt roads, which were seldom properly maintained following the rainy seasons. During a typical torrential rainstorm, many of these dirt roads would simply be washed away.

We conducted our evangelistic meetings in large outdoor markets in these remote villages. The markets were often filled with hundreds of people buying and selling goods. We would locate a good spot, set up our equipment and invite the people to gather to hear our message. The music attracted hundreds of people, so once the large crowd had gathered, we would preach the gospel

124

IN THE WAR

and invite them to surrender their lives to Jesus. In every meeting we witnessed hundreds of people surrendering their lives to Christ.

Though every campaign had memorable events, this campaign had one which I would never forget. We had been preaching all day outside of the city and as evening approached, our team planned to have one more meeting. The location that they selected was in the city, near a sawmill and several bars. As darkness fell, we set up our equipment and the music began drawing in an audience of several hundred people. Evening meetings attracted a fair number of intoxicated individuals and I noted that, as usual, and with the bars nearby, there were some in the audience. Often, those who were intoxicated would interrupt the meetings. However, this evening, things remained calm, at first.

When it came time for me to preach, my interpreter introduced me as I stepped up onto the platform and stood beside him. Occasionally, when the music stopped and the preaching began, some of the crowd would dissipate. However, I was pleased to see that this crowd remained for the entire message. During the time that we were preaching, there was an occasional stir in the audience by one of the intoxicated individuals, but the crowd remained attentive.

I finished my message and extended the invitation to repent and receive Jesus Christ. Several hundred people indicated their desire to repent so I prayed with all those who came forward. When I finished praying, I turned the meeting back to my team, who would conduct the immediate follow-up.

As I continued standing there, beside my interpreter, I noticed a man jumping over the boundary rope we had placed around the platform. The man began screaming and swearing at me in English. He also kept pointing his finger at me while he was screaming. I stepped down from the platform and walked over to him, intending to attempt to calm him down. I asked him why he was so angry at me. He screamed that I was a servant of Satan and a racist. I

125

BOB MCLAUGHLIN

assured him I was not a racist and that I represented Jesus Christ, not Satan. I asked him to stop screaming obscenities and interrupting the meeting. I knew the entire audience was watching this whole scenario.

It was obvious to me that this man was unwilling to listen to my pleas. I decided that I needed to pray for him, so while he continued to scream, I dropped to my knees in front of him and began to pray out loud. Sadly, this made him even angrier, and his rage reached a point where he swung his fist and punched me in the head. The impact caused me to lean slightly to one side, but fortunately, it didn't knock me unconscious. As I struggled to stand up, I heard the crowd shouting in unison in their Chichewa language. The man who had struck me literally jumped the rope and ran into the darkness, while a group of men chased after him and the crowd continued chanting the same thing over and over.

My team approached me and asked if I was hurt. I assured them that I was fine and then asked them what the crowd was chanting and why the man ran away. Once they realized I really was fine, they began to laugh. They told me that the man sealed his fate when he punched me. I asked what that meant. They replied that the crowd was chanting to the man that now he was crocodile meat, for hitting a white man. I said I hoped they wouldn't kill him. They laughed again and told me that if they caught him, they really might throw him to the crocodiles. I felt so bad that I prayed hard for that man.

Later that evening, I realized it probably was not such a good idea to bow in prayer, with my eyes closed, right in front of that angry man. Perhaps, as one friend told me later, it might be best to always keep an eye open in such cases.

To this day, I do not know if that man became crocodile meat or if he was able to escape. Only God knows. However, I will never forget those words, "You are crocodile meat."

Chapter 18

THE BULLWHIP AND NATIONAL TELEVISION NEWS

In my peripheral vision, I couldn't help but notice a man walking rapidly on the far-left side of the auditorium. He appeared to be carrying either a large rope or a coiled wire in one hand. A few prison guards were stationed along the back wall, listening to our program. Because the guards didn't react as the man rushed towards the stairs leading onto the platform, I assumed there was nothing to be concerned about and kept on preaching.

Two and a half weeks earlier I had flown into the city of Kazan, on the Volga River in Russia, and boarded the large mission ship. I had been invited by my Finnish evangelist friend and the parachurch organization he was affiliated with. Their US office had scheduled many opportunities for me to preach in cities along the river.

Unfortunately, soon after my arrival, I learned that all my scheduled bookings to preach had been mysteriously cancelled. So, the Russian leaders did the best they could to arrange several preaching engagements for me during those days.

We left the large ship and drove to the prison for one of the preaching engagements. Thankfully we arrived early, as the registration process for all visitors was detailed and lengthy. Also, it was unusual for a music group, with women, to minister in this all-men's prison, making the visit a bit riskier.

The large prison had razor wire and armed guards all along the top of the walls. We parked our vehicles and made our way to the entrance of the prison where the guards came out to check on us. Once they realized who we were and why we were there, they opened the large gates, and we were escorted by armed guards to the warden's office. We were taken through a series of fenced-in pathways with more razor wire curled on the top of the fences. The warden greeted us, and we began the long registration process.

When that was finished, we were taken through a series of tunnels and more fenced-in pathways to a large hall, where there were over five hundred men gathered, waiting for us to arrive and to present our program. When we entered the hall, we noticed that the guards seemed to show disapproval of our presence. The prisoners sat, with sad and glum faces, as they watched us go to the platform. At this point, I noticed that there was a Russian TV crew sitting in the front row. *How interesting*, I thought.

Our program began with a Russian music team from Saint Petersburg giving a beautiful performance. Their music was used by the Lord in a powerful way, as the glum and sad looks of the men dissipated with each beautiful number. The thunderous applause after every song indicated the prisoners' appreciation. In addition to singing, each member of the music group gave a short testimony between songs.

I sat in my chair, praying that God would soften the hearts of these hardened and desperate criminals, and save their souls. As I saw many of the prisoners becoming emotional and crying, it was clear to me that the audience was ready to hear the gospel.

Eventually, the leader of the music team introduced me, and I, along with my interpreter, made our way up the steps and onto the platform. Once again, the men applauded loudly, and we

IN THE WAR

began by thanking them for allowing us to be with them. They applauded again.

The interpreter assigned to me was Leo, a young university student from the city of Kazan. He spoke excellent English and was studying in northern Italy to be a scientist. He was a highly intelligent and pleasant young man, as well as a dedicated born-again Christian. I mention this because at times in the past, I had used interpreters who were not born-again believers, but none the less, were excellent interpreters.

Leo stood on my right, about five feet away from me, and together we preached a simple gospel message with great authority, through the power of the Holy Spirit. The audience was extremely attentive.

Before long, we were nearing the point where I would extend an invitation for those, who desired to repent and receive Christ, to come forward. This was when I noticed the man coming down the aisle, on my left, carrying what looked like either coiled wire or a rope. I did not realize that he had gone behind the stage curtain and had come out onto the platform behind us. Just as I was about to give the invitation, there was an extremely loud crack right beside my head. It was so startling that I jumped and nearly dropped my Bible. I turned towards my interpreter, noting that he too had been startled, and we looked at each other, wondering what had just happened! A moment passed and we heard another loud crack. Then both of us realized that there was a man cracking a large bullwhip between us. Once he knew that we saw him, he began shouting as he continued to crack the whip near my head.

I asked my interpreter what the man was shouting. Leo replied that he was saying that this is Mother Russia, and I have been sent from hell so the men should not listen to me. Apparently, the man was Russian Orthodox and devotedly opposed to evangelicalism.

The leader of the music group came onto the platform and said to me, "This could become a dangerous situation."

129

BOB MCLAUGHLIN

"Well, how can we shut this guy up?" I asked.

"Hand him the microphone!" he answered. I learned years ago to trust my national friends, so I looked the man in the eyes and handed it to him. I was astonished as he took the microphone, calmly made a few comments, and then handed it back to me. He coiled up the bullwhip in his hand, walked off the platform and took a seat at the back of the auditorium.

I surveyed the hall and noticed that the guards had not budged from their posts during the entire ordeal. I also noted that the TV crew had been filming the whole event.

At this point, I decided it was necessary, due to the uniqueness of the interruption, to give a quick overview of the message we had delivered. Once we finished the overview, I extended the invitation to repent and receive Christ. Over fifty men made their way forward and humbly stood in front of the platform. They bowed their heads and prayed to receive Jesus Christ into their hearts.

When the prayer was over, we were quickly led out of the hall to the applause of the prisoners. The warden and two grumpy looking guards escorted us to the front gate. I thanked the warden for allowing us the privilege of speaking to the men. I shook his hand and we departed from the prison. When we arrived back at the ship, we rejoiced over the salvation of many of the prisoners. My Russian friends told me that most likely there were many others who prayed to receive Christ but did not want to come forward for fear of persecution from Russian Orthodox prisoners, who abused fellow inmates with leanings toward evangelicalism. They also talked of the protection that clearly came from the Lord, noting that the guards had done absolutely nothing to intervene and protect us during the entire ordeal with the bullwhip. Once again, they emphasized just how potentially dangerous the meeting had been. I agreed.

Several weeks later I returned to Russia for another evangelistic campaign. I flew into Saint Petersburg where I was met by

IN THE WAR

one of my Russian friends. Together we flew to Chita, in far eastern Siberia, with a brief stop in the city of Omsk to change aircrafts.

As our Aeroflot jetliner taxied to the gate, I noticed a TV crew, with microphones, on the tarmac. I surmised that there must be someone of importance on the plane, who they were waiting to interview. Jokingly, I turned to my Russian friend and asked, "Is President Yeltsin on this plane?"

He looked at me and said, "No, the TV crew is for you!"

Astonished, I exclaimed, "Come on! No way!"

"It's true, Bob," he said, "You are now semi famous here in Russia because of the incident in the prison a few weeks ago."

"How so?" I asked. He told me that the Russian TV crew had filmed the entire incident of the bullwhip in the prison, and apparently aired it on national television throughout Russia.

As I deplaned, I thought about how amazing our God is.

The first question the TV reporter asked me was, "Mr. McLaughlin, may I ask you if you were afraid in the prison when the man was cracking his whip near your head?"

"No," I answered, "Just confused."

She continued, "Mr. McLaughlin, do you fear being back in Russia?"

Again, I responded with a firm "No! I feel it is an honor to be back again in Russia."

Then she asked, "Would you be afraid to return to that prison?"

"Not at all," I responded. "As a matter of fact, I would like very much to return to that prison."

"If you returned, what is the first thing you would want to do?" she asked.

I smiled and said, "I would want to meet with the man who had the bullwhip and tell him how much Jesus loves him." The reporter concluded by thanking me for telling the Russian people how much they are loved by God.

Once again, I was in awe at the amazing intervention of God: how He took a potentially dangerous event and used it for His glory and to enlarge our ministry throughout Russia. Because of the television news report, our ministry became known, and we received more invitations to preach.

King David said, *"The Lord encamps around those who fear Him, and rescues them."* (Psalm 34:7 NASB)

2 Thessalonians 3:3 says, *"But the Lord is faithful, and He will strengthen and protect you from the evil one."* (NASB)

Russian T.V. and Radio Interviews

IN THE WAR

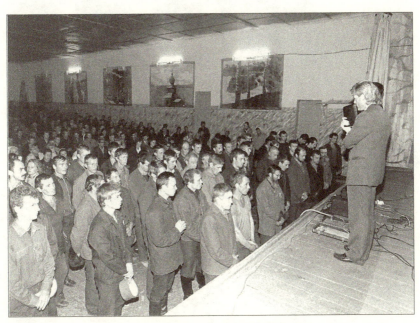

Preaching in Russian Prison

Chapter 19

A Siberian Adventure

I was excited to return to Siberia again. As my plane began its descent into the city of Chita, I was thankful that it was summer. I recalled just how cold it had been in Chita during my previous ministry, held in the dead of winter. On this, my third campaign in that area, I was accompanied by an interpreter and a soloist from Saint Petersburg. I was looking forward to working, once again, in cooperation with the Chita Baptist Church. This church, like many I was privileged to work with in Russia, had a vision and a goal to evangelize and plant new churches in areas they had prayed for. So, the leadership was pleased with our willingness to go wherever they wanted us to minister.

Though I was glad it was summertime, I was still unprepared and surprised, as we came off the plane, to feel just how warm (and even hot at times) it was in Chita. After we collected our bags, we were met by our Russian pastor friends and their wives. They took us to our hotel to check in, and then to the Baptist church where we met with other church leaders to discuss the particulars of this unique mission.

Once we arrived at the church, we were served coffee and a snack before we got down to talking about the upcoming trip. The leaders rolled out a large map and used it to point out the overall mission. To say I was excited would be an understatement, as I listened to them share the scope and vision they had for this challenging campaign.

Arrangements had been made for us to rent a large boat, along with its captain and first officer, to take us on a lengthy trip up the Shilka River, which flowed northeast, past the city of Chita. The plan was for us to conduct evangelistic meetings in seventeen villages all along the banks of the river. This boat was to become our home away from home for many days so we would be eating and sleeping on the boat. Once we had finished the river trip, we would be flying by helicopter to a remote village, the last stop of our mission.

According to our Russian friends, many of these villages had no gospel witness, and they believed that no one had ever attempted this type of a mission, with an effort to reach the villagers with the gospel.

We finished our planning meeting and then prayed together that God would pour out His Spirit on us and bless and protect us. We also prayed that the mission would be a complete success. After we enjoyed having dinner with the church leaders we were dropped off at our hotel for the night. Before going to sleep that night, I thanked God for the awesome privilege to preach the gospel again in Siberia.

Our vehicle arrived the next morning after breakfast and we were taken to the banks of the river to wait for our boat. Several hours passed, and still there was no sign of the boat. I was assured that it would arrive, and we would set sail on our exotic mission.

Eventually, the boat arrived, and we were introduced to Captain Yuri and his first officer, Vasyli. We loaded our belongings and began our journey on the massive, muddy-looking, winding Shilka River that stretched several hundred miles to China. The boat was about forty feet long and ten feet wide with benches on each side, which we used as beds. In the very back of the boat I had a small office,

IN THE WAR

so to speak, with a desk and chair. I spent many hours in that office during our trip. When the weather was pleasant, we often spent time on the roof, basking in the sun.

As we journeyed down the river, our approach was to mount our sound system speakers on the roof of the boat as we came near each village. Once the system and microphones were ready, we would start our generator, and the captain would slowly sail past the village, while my interpreter announced our intentions to the people. Then the boat would be turned around and we sailed past the village going the other way. This allowed us to announce again who we were and why we were visiting their village. Following the second announcement, our captain would slowly bring the boat to shore and dock it.

This, of course, caused quite a stir in the village and we would see people coming out of their homes and running down the paths towards the water's edge. Young and old alike began gathering on the shore to see what all the commotion was about. To my utter amazement, some of the people brought chairs and crates and sat themselves down just a few feet away from the front of the boat, while others simply stood or sat on the grass or rocks. Our soloist would give a few words of greeting and then begin to minister in song.

The obvious excitement of the people was utterly contagious. They would show their appreciation with loud clapping and shouts of glee. The children would giggle and squeal as they shared their joy with each other. It was truly a sight to behold.

After the music was done, my interpreter would then introduce me and together we stood in the stern of the boat and preached the gospel. I remember thinking about the story in scripture of how Jesus also preached from a boat.

The people were always so attentive, and many would cry during my message. I told them how much God loved them and that He wanted to forgive their sin. I explained how they could repent

137

BOB MCLAUGHLIN

of their sin and surrender their hearts to Christ. When I would give the invitation to come forward, nearly all the village people would come as close as possible to the boat, and humbly bow and pray to receive Christ. This amazing response was repeated in every village.

Eventually, word somehow traveled before us to the other villages, so in the coming days, as we went from one village to another, we were often surprised to see many people already gathered on the shore. Yet, just to be cautious, we would announce ourselves as we sailed back and forth before docking. As a result, we didn't have any trouble and we found that our ministry in these villages was well received. Village leaders would greet us with a round-shaped, freshly baked loaf of bread. On the top of the bread sat a small cup or container of salt. In some villages we were invited to come ashore and have our meeting in the village square. Before we would set sail, the women of the village would bring us meals for our journey, like large pots of soup with freshly baked bread and broiled fish. Then, as we sailed away, the entire village would come to the shore and wave as they shouted, "Slava Bogu" and "spaseba" which in English is, "Praise God," and "thank you." They would continue this until we were out of sight.

When the captain docked our boat for the night, we had an opportunity to take care of some of our personal needs. We would wash our clothes in the river and hang them up to dry throughout the interior of the boat. Some evenings we would build a campfire to heat our food and enjoy dinner together on the shore. As darkness fell, we would make our beds on the benches and go off to sleep for the night.

We ended our river ministry at the town of Mogocha, where we had a successful evangelistic meeting. Next, we were driven to a very small village called Tupik, and once again, the church planting was a success. The small cabin we were given for our accommodations was a nice change from living on the boat.

138

IN THE WAR

After spending a couple of days in Tupik, we were to fly by helicopter to a remote trapping village called Alokma. The helicopter
made a monthly flight there to drop off supplies and pick up furs
to transport back to Chita.

My Russian friends informed me that the cost of our return flight
to Alokma had been prearranged by the Chita pastors. However, as
was often the case, once we were ready to travel, the price had suddenly skyrocketed by a couple thousand US dollars. This resulted
in a rather lengthy and somewhat heated discussion between us
and the office manager of the helicopter. Thankfully, we were able
to negotiate a slightly higher price with just a few more US dollars
than was originally agreed upon. We were instructed to wait for
the helicopter in a nearby pasture, where we ended up waiting for
more than an hour and even got sunburned. Eventually, and thankfully, our helicopter arrived, and we were introduced to the pilots.

We loaded up all our equipment and began our flight into the
extremely remote, northern Siberian countryside. It was a beautiful sunny and clear day, so the pilots, who spoke good English,
invited me to join them in the cockpit. They pointed out the vast
territory covered in fir trees and said, "Bob, look! This is beautiful
Siberia. Do you like?" I replied that, indeed, it was beautiful, and I
liked it very much.

After more than an hour of flying, they pointed out the small,
remote trapping village of Alokma, off in the distance. They told
me that, once we landed, we would have a full hour to conduct our
program. They also stressed that we could not take longer than
an hour because they needed to drop us off in Tupik before flying
on to the city of Chita. I assured them that we could complete our
program in an hour.

The pilots skillfully brought our helicopter down for a very soft
landing on the landing pad which, frankly, was poorly constructed
of two by sixes, many of which were warped and rotted. Of course,
the entire village saw that we were coming, and they were already

139

gathering around the landing pad. We quickly jumped out and unloaded all our equipment. Within just five minutes we set up our speakers and microphones, started our generator, and were ready to begin. The chief of the village welcomed us and thanked us for coming. I asked him how many people lived in his village. He replied that there were one hundred and forty-eight men, women and children. I thanked him for giving us permission to speak to his entire village.

My interpreter introduced us and then our soloist ministered in music to the appreciative audience. As the soloist sang, I stood under the blades of the helicopter and prayed that many would repent and give their hearts to Christ. During my prayer, I was emotionally struck with the reality of what was unfolding right before my eyes. I continued to pray, "Oh my, Lord! You are so amazing because You have brought us hundreds of miles into the vast, Siberian countryside to this little, out of the way village, with one all-consuming purpose – to give these people the opportunity to hear your message of love and mercy for them."

Following the ministry of music, we preached the gospel through the power of the Holy Spirit. After my short sermon, I gave the invitation, inviting all who desired to repent and receive Christ to come forward and bow their heads in prayer. Immediately, many people came and stood in front of us and received Jesus into their hearts. My interpreter did the basic follow-up and assured the people of Alokma that every month, the pastors from Chita would return by helicopter to conduct a service for their newly formed church.

When it was time to leave, the people helped us load our equipment and then, with tears of deep appreciation, they thanked us for coming. As the helicopter lifted off the landing pad, I looked out of the window and waved goodbye to those dear people. Once we were high above the village, I wept at all that had just happened. To this day, many years later, I can still see the entire village of Alokma waving goodbye until we were out of sight. As we flew back to Tupik, we spent time praying and praising God for all He had done.

We spent the night in Tupik and the next day we were driven back to Mogocha. Our boat was waiting for us, so we loaded up and sailed back to Chita. When we reported to the Baptist church about all that God had done, they were extremely excited at the success of the entire campaign. Our team reported that we had recorded a total of 1,390 publicly indicated decisions for Christ during the mission. On our long flight to Moscow, we also prepared a report for the president of the Russian Baptist Union.

A few days later I boarded my flight back to Canada. As I flew over the Atlantic Ocean, I was nearly overwhelmed with the fact that I had just completed a Siberian adventure.

Shilka River Siberia Boat Team

Announcing arrival in village

They gather at the shore

Welcome with bread and salt

Response to the Gospel

Village Fisherman and Bob

Our helicopter to remote Siberia

IN THE WAR

Response to the preaching

Bob and Leo in Red Square

Bob in the Ukraine

Chapter 20

YOU ARE AN ANSWER TO PRAYER

I was on one of my many ministry campaigns to the Philippines. After a long, tiring flight to Manila, I spent the night in the city before flying on to Mindanao, the large island in the southern region of the Philippines. The next morning, I flew into Davao City, Mindanao, where I was met by the national team I would be ministering with over the next three weeks. Once we retrieved my luggage, we began our long drive to Malita, a large fishing town on the east coast of the big island. Upon our arrival, we met with missionary friends for dinner and an overnight stay before continuing our mission.

The next day dawned clear and extremely hot. By 10:00 AM we were on our way to the beach. We hired a few young boys from the village to help with the unloading of all our bags from our jeepney onto the thirty-foot pump boat. The pump boat, typically used throughout the Philippines, was approximately five feet wide with a small cabin. Pontoons on either side helped to stabilize the craft from capsizing in high seas.

Once our equipment and supplies were loaded, and my teammates had waded out to the boat, it was now my turn to get on board. My Filipino friends broke out in laughter as I waded in chest-deep water to the side of the boat. With each wave the boat would lift and then drop down once the wave passed. Considering this was my first time boarding such a craft, and my only lesson was watching the others, I thought I was doing rather well. The process of boarding a pump boat involved precise timing of the waves. My assistant, who was experienced in this, helped to hoist me up when the waves were at their low point. Once I was on board, the team cheered, and I too joined in the laughter.

After all the laughing, teasing, and joking had died down, I asked one of the pastors to lead us in prayer. This elderly man, who hailed from Digos City, volunteered to come along to help with follow-up in our evangelistic campaigns. Following his prayer, we set sail on the beautiful, sparkling, blue ocean. Our captain maneuvered us out to sea several hundred meters offshore and, at last, we were finally on our way. This campaign would take us to many remote fishing villages along the eastern coast of Mindanao. We sailed at maximum speed over the four to five-foot swells. It really was a wonderful journey, but it was blistering hot and I sunburned badly.

Our pump boat captain began sharing stories of piracy, which he claimed was quite common along this coast. He also pointed to the shore and the mountains, commenting that New People's Army (NPA) guerrillas were in those mountains. I asked him to explain in detail what to expect should we encounter a hijacking by pirates. He laughed and said, "They will likely kill us, but may allow you to swim to shore." Then with more laughter he added, "But then once you are ashore, you will most likely be captured by the NPA."

Another man shouted to me, laughing and jeering, "Swimming to shore could prove deadly too, if attacked by sharks." I knew there was some truth in these comments, and though we laughed, we were all on alert.

With each wave, the saltwater spray covered everything on the boat, including us. We sailed down the coast for a few hours, eventually reaching our first venue – a small fishing village, right on the shore.

IN THE WAR

Many young men from the village quickly gathered on the beach to assist us in unloading our equipment. The captain had to carefully maneuver our boat to shore, making sure he beached it without hitting coral and the many jagged rocks beneath the surface. Timing was the key to successfully bringing the boat in safely. To accomplish this, the captain would catch a carefully preselected wave. His many years of experience enabled him to skillfully move the craft safely near the shore, bringing the nose as close as possible to the beach. Once we were in position, the young men waded out to the side of the boat, and we offloaded all the equipment to them. One by one, they fought the waves in the chest-deep water, reached up to take an item from the boat, placed it on their shoulders and then waded back to the shore. This was repeated until the boat was completely unloaded, and then it was my turn to go. I jumped into the warm, tropical water and slowly made my way through the waves.

Once I reached the shore, I could not help but notice a man running towards me, waving his arms and shouting, "Praise God!" He ran up to me, wrapped his arms around me and said, "I am Pastor June. Please come quickly. You are an answer to prayer. We must go to my father's home." I asked if I could first change out of my wet clothes, to which he replied, "Yes, but we must hurry." As I put on some dry clothes, June began to share his story with me.

"When I was a very little boy, of about four years of age, my mother abandoned me. She placed me on a pump boat, and I was dropped off at this very village. For one reason or another, but very often when parents could not afford to keep their children, they would pay a boat captain to leave their child at one of the villages far down the coast."

As cruel as this seems – it was common practice. His story captivated my full attention.

He continued, "Thankfully, a kind woman saw me crying on the beach and took pity on me. She took me home and she and

149

BOB MCLAUGHLIN

her husband adopted me. My new home was that of the most successful businessman in the village – a coconut plantation owner."

A few years later, when June was sixteen years old, he had an encounter with Jesus and got saved. He immediately began sharing his new faith in Christ with his adopted parents. Though they loved their son they repeatedly rejected his pleas to receive Jesus as their Savior. Eventually, his father became rather tired of June's repeated attempts to witness to him, so he gave his son the following challenge, "June, you claim your God is a God of miracles and He answers your prayers. I will repent and receive your Jesus, but only if He meets my request."

June replied, "Yes, my God hears my prayers and answers them. What is your request? How can I pray?"

Smirking, his adopted father said, "I will repent and receive your Jesus if and only if God brings an American preacher to my home."

June responded, "OK, I will pray that God will send an American preacher to your home." As June walked away, he hoped his smirking father would not detect his concern and frustration with such a most difficult request.

He continued his story, "I began crying out to God, laying that humanly impossible request before Him."

June admitted to me that he was disappointed in his father's request and had hoped for an easier one to lay before God. However, he prayed faithfully day after day, while the days stretched into weeks and months and then years. As time passed – seemingly unending – he became discouraged, and at times, angry. On occasion, he would ask God why his father would demand such a request and each time, he would come to the obvious conclusion – his adopted parents never expected this request to be met.

June's parents often took joy in realizing that, as the years passed, God did not answer their son's prayer. At times, they would taunt him, that is, until the day I saw him running towards me on the beach.

150

IN THE WAR

June prayed faithfully for more than twenty-five years that God would send an American preacher to his parents' home, so his excitement was obvious and for good reason! After all, in direct answer to those prayers, God sent me, an American preacher, to this village and to June's father's home.

We arrived at the rather large, thatched roof and bamboo home. I remember the expression of shock and disbelief on the faces of the old Filipino and his wife when they opened the door. They were speechless for a few moments. June, of course, was grinning from ear to ear. I also recall seeing tears in their aging eyes as June introduced me and my interpreter.

We were invited to sit in the big room where we were served refreshments. Following all the formal greetings and small talk, June's father gave some instructions to his young servant. Apparently, he told him to go and stop all work on the plantation and in the mill and invite all the employees to the big room. They all came in, wondering why they had been summoned to the owner's home. June told me later that for them to be invited into the home all at the same time was unheard of. In fact, it would be rare for any of them to even be allowed into the house. However, on this rare occasion, once the workers had all entered the room, they were served a cool drink and instructed to sit quietly and listen to a message from God, through the American evangelistic preacher.

I was amazed at the events that unfolded before my eyes. It was incredible to see these people sitting all around the big room and curiously looking at me. As I recall, besides me and my interpreter, there were about fourteen employees present, two house servants, as well as June and his parents. June's father, who spoke through my interpreter, instructed me to tell everyone gathered there about Jesus. It was an amazing and totally unexpected opportunity. The room fell silent, and all eyes were focused on me. It was truly a beautiful God-Moment.

151

I wasted no time in preaching the Gospel to the eighteen unbelievers gathered in the big room. When I gave the invitation to repent and receive Christ, all eighteen, including June's adopted parents, prayed one by one to repent and receive Jesus that day!

As we were leaving, June's father told me that he was amazed God brought me to his home and that he really did not think it would ever happen. He said, "When I saw you at my door, I knew God sent you and that I must receive Jesus today." I reminded him that God had answered June's faithful prayers. He agreed, smiling broadly, and that smile said it all: *You are an answer to prayer.*

A remote tribe in the Philippines

Chapter 21

CLOSE CALL IN MINDANAO

We had just completed the last and most fruitful evangelistic meeting of the entire Maragusan campaign, held in the barrio of Maglagoney, the Philippines. Maragusan is a town, high in the mountains overlooking the Compostela Valley on the island of Mindanao, and Maglagoney is a community, known as a "barrio," of that town. Much of the area is jungle and traveling by Jeep to Maragusan was dangerous. The so-called roads we traveled were not what one might picture in their mind; they were badly constructed roads winding up the mountainside.

That Sunday night, over five hundred people had gathered on and around the basketball court to watch The Jesus Film and to hear us preach the gospel of Jesus Christ. As was our practice when showing The Jesus Film, someone would give their testimony during the changing of the reels. That night Trudy gave a beautiful testimony explaining clearly how she came to have a personal relationship with Jesus. As I listened to her, I was so incredibly happy to have her with me and, what made it even more special was that this was her very first trip to the Philippines.

Another custom when showing The Jesus Film was that our projectionist would stop the film right at the crucifixion of Christ and I would then preach the gospel. My interpreter that night was Pastor Carlos Fajardo and together we preached with great power and authority. When we gave the invitation to repent and come forward to receive Christ, the response was immediate. Within two to three minutes, over four hundred people flooded across the basketball court and stood humbly at the front of our platform. As I looked deep into their faces, I could see many who were in tears. We proceeded to lead them in a prayer of repentance, which they prayed out loud, together. It was a glorious moment.

Following the basic counseling and follow-up by our team, we packed up our equipment, loaded the Jeep and drove to Pastor Carlos' home, located near Maragusan.

Our hearts were full of gratitude to our Lord for the amazing, successful, evangelistic campaign we had just completed. As our team sat around the late-night dinner table with Pastor Carlos, our host, we all agreed that this campaign was, by far, the best one we had ever conducted in the Philippines. Our calculations showed that we had preached in thirteen barrios and four high schools, where we witnessed a total of 4,210 publicly indicated decisions for Christ. An added blessing was that we also planted two churches in two of the barrios which church leaders desired to reach with the gospel.

Before retiring for the night, we spent time in praise and prayer to God for the successful campaign, giving Him all the glory, honor, and praise. As Trudy and I took our leave and went to bed, I was thinking about a conversation we had over two weeks ago, before flying to the Philippines.

"Where did you say we are going to minister in the Philippines?" Trudy asked.

I answered, "We will be ministering on the big island of Mindanao."

Trudy responded, "Isn't that a rather dangerous area of the world, these days?"

I looked at her and smiled as I said, "Sweetheart, God is our protector, and I don't think our friends indicated there would be

IN THE WAR

any trouble where we are going. Besides, I have been to Mindanao many times and I never had any real problems."

Shrugging her shoulders, Trudy replied with, "Well, I guess we will find out when we get there."

I smiled as I thought about that conversation and slipped into a deep sleep. Shortly after falling asleep, I was abruptly awakened by someone shouting – Carlos and Basilio were exchanging words with some strangers. I looked at the clock – it was 2:10 AM. Trudy also woke up and asked what was happening.

I whispered, "Hon, get dressed quickly. Something's not right!" Once the shouting stopped, I opened the door of our room and inquired what the problem was. Carlos and Basilio told us that it was potentially a dangerous situation. They said five armed men came to the door, demanding that they get the two Americans and the Jeep, with all the equipment. They said they needed us to drive them to Davao City, a five-hour drive on treacherous, unpaved, mountain passes. They claimed it was a matter of life and death. Carlos knew they were lying and that their intentions were to kidnap us for ransom. He told them to go away and leave the Americans alone. The men threatened him and said they would return in an hour.

Carlos told us that these men were more than likely members of the NPA, a Marxist rebel group, who for years had been fighting the Philippine government. He continued by telling us that over the last year, the NPA had used similar tactics in their area, with grave consequences. In some cases, not only were vehicles and motor bikes stolen, but their owners were murdered. He said that these NPA members had threatened him in the past and, with delight, told him that he was a target. At times they had also put a gun to his head.

It was now 3:00 AM and we heard the men returning, just as they promised. Pastor Carlos put us in a small room at the back of his house and told us to pray and not to come out until he told us to. I noticed, as he shut our door, that he was holding a .45 handgun.

155

Carlos and Basilio went outside to speak with the men. After fifteen minutes of tense negotiations, they came back inside and told us that the men were gone but had promised, once again, to return, and had threatened Carlos if he didn't comply with their demands. As we knelt in the small room in prayer, awaiting the return of the men, I told Trudy that I was sorry for putting her in such a terrible situation. Remaining amazingly calm, Trudy said, "Hon, don't worry. God is in control and if it is our time, then so be it. But I believe," she continued, "that the Lord will protect us." Frankly, I was amazed at her faith.

A few minutes later, only one man returned, unarmed, and told Carlos and Basilio that there wouldn't be any further trouble for us. The men never returned.

Later that morning, we had a great time of fellowship with the area pastors and their wives as well as all the local church people. Together we praised God for His protection and for all He had done during the entire evangelistic campaign.

We returned to Davao City and then flew home, our hearts full of gratitude to God. While on our flight home, I said to Trudy, "Well that was truly a close call in Mindanao."

The Psalmist proclaimed, *"I will say to the Lord, 'My refuge and my fortress, My God, in whom I trust!' For it is He who delivers you from the trapper..."* (Psalm 91:2-3a NASB)

PART FIVE
TRIALS, ADVERSITIES, & TRIBULATIONS TAKE THEIR TOLL

A PREAMBLE TO THIS SECTION

As mentioned in the preface of this book I pointed out that absolutely nothing happens in our lives apart from the will of God. This fact though difficult for us to understand is based on the theological doctrine of "meticulous providence" or "the greater good doctrine."

In this section, you will read chapters detailing various trials, tribulations, and adversities that our ministry encountered over the years.

Some readers will undoubtedly surmise that much of these that we encountered may have come about as a direct result of my ongoing secret sin of alcoholism at the time. This opinion has merit in that God clearly points out that He will not and cannot go back on His word. The book of Galatians states clearly, *"Do not be deceived, God is not mocked; for whatever a man sows, this he will also reap."* Galatians 6:7 (NASB).

Yet these things are a definite part of human life in general but especially for the Christian because of the spiritual battle being fought between good and evil.

As one reads the Bible you can clearly see how many people conspired against God's chosen. Allow me to list a few.

There is the story of Joseph's brothers who conspired to get rid of him because of their jealousy towards him. There was evil jealous Haman who desired to annihilate the entire Jewish population in Persia. Evil wicked Queen Jezebel and her entire royal family conspired to have the prophet Elijah murdered. The

Philistines conspired to have Sampson captured using Delilah to lie and deceive Sampson into telling her how to have his supernatural strength removed from him. There is the story of the wicked Egyptian Pharaoh who conspired to have all the Jewish boys killed. Nehemiah had much opposition, Danial faced being torn apart by real lions because of a conspiracy plotted against him. Daniel's three friends were conspired against and thrown into a furnace of fire. Even Judas one of Jesus's disciples betrayed Him and conspired with religious leaders for 30 pieces of silver. These are but a few Bible characters who faced various trials, tribulations, and adversities.

So, yes, I readily agree that some of these things in this section may have been a consequence to my hidden sin, however, you will read of clear opposition later in the last section of this book where those encounters take place long after my repentance.

Lastly, though God may have literally raised up these people in accordance with His will to cause such difficulties, it does not negate the sin they themselves committed in the process. They too will reap the consequences of their sin. Yet they can have hope because absolutely nothing (including these things) happens apart from the will of God. All that is required for things to turn around for their greater good is repentance.

Chapter 22

THE CHRISTIAN FARMER

I first met the 'Christian farmer' in 1980 while attending church in the lower mainland of British Columbia. He appeared to be a hardworking man with a rather gruff personality and a scruffy appearance. At the time, he owned a very profitable dairy farm. He, like many others in the BC lower mainland, would make an annual trip to the Hawaii. He drove a new car and a big Harley Davidson motorcycle. Like many successful Christian people, he enjoyed his toys and why not? He worked hard, loved the Lord, and gave generously of his finances, or so it seemed!

It wasn't until a few years later, when I was invited to preach in his home church, that he began taking a personal interest in our evangelistic ministry. That morning, when I gave the invitation to come to the front of the church for repentance, there was a tremendous response. Following the service, we were invited to the farmer's home for Sunday dinner. One of the first questions he had for me was, "Where did you get that message?" I told him that I had received it from the Lord. He indicated to me that he was very impressed with the message and the response, and that he felt they would like to participate in our ministry. He shared with us how they were generously supporting a TV evangelist and would like to help our ministry as well. Over the next few years, he became very involved in our work.

He was an unusual character in that he had a very strange way about him when it came to financially supporting the ministry. I first discovered this when I phoned him with the challenge to pray about donating $700.00 towards a flight ticket, I needed for a ministry trip to Europe. "Well, how much do you need for the whole trip?" he questioned. I told him approximately $1400.00 would cover it. "Why don't you ask me for the entire amount? You need to be bolder and more up-front about your needs!" he almost shouted.

"Well, OK," I said, "would you like to donate $1400.00?" Laughing, he replied, "No, I'm only going to give you $700.00. Let that be a lesson to you. The next time you have a need, ask me for the full amount." I sensed that he enjoyed the control factor. Now, don't misunderstand me here. I have always been grateful for any donations to the ministry. I just don't appreciate it when people play power games with me – especially head games regarding giving. However, this incident pales in comparison to what happened later.

When the telephone rang in my office in the winter of 1990-1991, I answered, and the Christian farmer was on the line. He and his family had recently sold their dairy farm and moved to a different province, where they now owned an exceptionally large turkey farm and were prospering very well. Following the usual 'how's things,' he said, "I've decided to purchase a newer vehicle for you."

"Are you really sure about this?" I questioned.

"Yes, and here's what I expect you to do," was his answer. The farmer had specific guidelines, but no mention with regards to cost; I was to simply follow his instructions.

The guidelines given were very specific and demanding. We were to drive to Saskatoon, Saskatchewan the following weekend and go directly to a specific dealership in that city. We were to seek out a specific salesman employed at the dealership, introduce

IN THE WAR

ourselves and tell him who had sent us and why we were there. We were to spend as much time as necessary with the salesman to find a vehicle suitable for our needs. Once all this was completed, the carefully selected automobile would then be paid for by the farmer. I wrote down all the instructions carefully and crosschecked them with him. Then I said, "You know I really don't know a lot about automobiles?"

With a laugh he answered, "That's why I'm sending you to this man. He will help you select the car that's right for you!" Little did I know that he was setting me up.

A few days later our girls went with Trudy and me for the weekend. We drove the two and a half hours to Saskatoon, checked into a hotel and went immediately to the dealership.

I followed the instructions to the letter. We spent that afternoon and evening looking over various cars, then returned the following morning and continued our search into the early afternoon. By this time, we had narrowed it down to two vehicles. The salesman strongly suggested we go with the newer one because, for the money, it was by far the better deal. However, since it was more expensive, I told the salesman that I really felt I needed to talk with the farmer before we made any deal.

The salesman took us into his office and called the Christian farmer. I spoke with him and informed him that his friend had helped us narrow it down to two vehicles, and I wanted him and the salesman to make the decision for us. I told him how thankful we were that he would do this for us, but that I was extremely uncomfortable making the final decision. "Yah, yah, OK, what are they asking for each car?" he inquired. I told him the price of each vehicle and that his friend was strongly suggesting that the more expensive one was the better deal for the money because it was only a year old and a demo car with very low mileage. "Yah, well you make the decision," was his response. I told him again that I would feel more comfortable if he and his salesman friend made

163

the decision. I said I wanted the salesman to explain the pros and cons of each vehicle and say which one he thought the farmer should buy for us, and why. I told him that I was going to give the phone back to his friend and once they had discussed it thoroughly to his satisfaction, I would go with the car that they both thought we should have. I then handed the phone back to the salesman.

Trudy and I waited there in his office and heard every word of the salesman's side of the conversation. We heard him quote the price of each vehicle along with what his expert opinion was regarding each one. We heard him answer 'yes' and 'no' to various questions. We heard him say, "Yes, it's the better deal by far for your money," and then, "OK, I'll tell him. Goodbye." We fully expected him to tell us which vehicle the Christian farmer had decided to purchase for us.

The salesman hung up the phone, turned to us and said with a smile, "It's a done deal! He said he'll go with the one you decide on."

"What was his choice?" I questioned.

"The decision is up to you," he replied. "He'll go along with the one you think is best." I was shocked. How could they not understand that we wanted them to make the decision? My thoughts were interrupted by the salesman. "Look," he continued, "My friend said for you to pick. Don't be foolish, take the best one. He would!!" I felt we needed to pray about it, so Trudy, the girls and I gathered outside for a time of prayer.

We went back in, and I asked the salesman again, "What did your friend say?"

"He said the decision is yours, and he will go along with the one you choose."

I looked at Trudy and said, "If he were buying this car for himself, which one would he buy?"

She answered, "The best one – without a question."

I stood there thinking back to the Christian farmer's comments to me regarding his belief that I should be "bold and up front"

IN THE WAR

about our needs. I remembered that he gave $700.00 as opposed to $1400.00 simply because I asked for a donation of $700.00, when the full need was $1400.00. I also remembered that he said, "Let that be a lesson to you." Once I finished reminiscing, while my poor girls fidgeted, I thought there was no way I could go wrong by choosing the better car. *Clearly that is what he wants me to do*, I reasoned. I turned to Trudy and said, "OK, let's just do it."

She responded with, "That's what he would do."

I then turned to the salesman and said, "OK, how do we go about buying the newer car?"

The salesman smiled with relief and commented, "You really have made the right decision." He continued, "Your friend said to buy the one you want, and he would make the payments."

At this point, we were committed, and felt like we had made the right decision. Now, the first thing I had to do was phone our bank and speak with the manager, who was familiar with the way we operated, since we had dealt strictly with him from the inception of our ministry. I remember how excited I was when I informed him that a friend was buying us a newer car.

He said, "Well, that seems rather unusual, I have never heard of such a thing." I remember thinking: *what a great testimony this is to my banker friend. It clearly demonstrates how benevolent and loving Christians are towards each other.* My thoughts of how wonderful this situation was, were interrupted by the bank manager's question, "OK, Bob, do you have your check book with you?"

I said, "Yes."

He continued, "Make out a check for the full amount, give it to the salesman and we will cover it. Then, come straight here to the bank and we'll do the paperwork. Congratulations Bob, I'm happy for you and your family."

We wrote a check for the full amount and completed all the necessary paperwork, which included trading in our car towards the purchase of the newer one. Once the paperwork was completed,

165

we took the licence plates from our old car and put them on the new car. We shook hands with the salesman and thanked him for his patience and understanding over the last couple of days. Before we drove out of the garage, he assured us once again that we had made the right decision. We returned to our hotel to check out and then drove the two and a half hours to the bank.

I will never forget the excitement and joy we all had in our hearts. I remember telling the girls that this is the way God works. He put a desire in the heart of the Christian farmer to meet our need for a more reliable car for our coast-to-coast trips. We decided to spend some time praying for that farmer and his family, so much of our drive to the bank was filled with praise and prayers of thanksgiving to our God. In fact, we were still singing Christian choruses when we finally pulled into the bank parking lot. I remember looking in the rear-view mirror at our two girls and thinking how this was such a great testimony to them. I knew they would never forget that day; I was so right!

We walked into the bank and asked for the manager. He approached us and said, "The loan manager is waiting for you." Then he continued, "She has received a call from your friend who's paying for your new car, and there seems to be a little snag we need to deal with."

We all walked into the loan manager's office and took a seat. We were grinning from ear to ear – she was not! With her jaw set in a stern position she said, "I received a call from your friend, and he is not willing to pay for the entire loan."

The words cut deep into my heart, and I thought, *wow, wait just a minute here. There must be a mistake of some kind.* I sat there confused and finally voiced the words, "I'm sorry, what did you say?"

"He's not willing to pay the full amount," she responded sternly, almost with a sneer.

I replied, "There has to be a mistake here."

"There is no mistake," she said, "He will not pay the full amount."

IN THE WAR

"What else did he say?" I asked. She leaned back in her office chair and told me the amount he was willing to pay. I'm sure I must have looked rather dumbfounded, sitting there with egg all over my face and with the annoying thought that I was in a very embarrassing situation, racing through my mind. My wife was looking at me, my girls were looking at me and I could feel the hot searing glare of the loan manager. I was extremely uncomfortable. Once again, I found myself speaking, basically repeating over and over, "There has to be some kind of a misunderstanding here, how can this be?" Then I addressed the loan manager, "OK, this really is confusing to us because the amount you say he is willing to pay is even less than the cheaper car that he said he would buy for us." In my heart I was thinking: *How could this be? Is it a deliberate willful attempt to embarrass us? What must my bank manager be thinking?* I continued, "The man buying the car for us was willing to pay for the car in its entirety. Oh, my goodness what kind of mess did I get myself into this time?" I stood to my feet and said, "OK, the whole thing is off, and we need to get this car back to the dealer before they sell the car we traded for this thing."

The loan manager countered, "Mr. McLaughlin, we can work out an additional loan for you, so you can keep the car."

I responded with, "There is no way we can afford to do that, we just don't have the money to pay for a loan. There has been a mistake, and we need to get this car back right away. Thank you for your time."

We got up to go and once more she said, "I'm sure we can work something out." I answered again that we needed to go – and we left.

The drive back to Saskatoon was totally different than the drive down. We were noticeably quiet and confused. The girls were asking questions that we could not answer. I just could not understand what had happened that day. The Christian farmer had clearly said he was going to buy the car that we finally decided on, and this was confirmed again and again. *So, was this a joke or*

167

something? Did the salesman mislead us? Did the farmer mislead us? I was at a loss for the answers to these and many other questions racing through my head. Now my goal was to get back to the dealership as fast as possible, praying that the salesman had not already sold our trade-in.

The closer we got to Saskatoon, the more uncomfortable I felt about the whole scenario. How embarrassing it was going to be to return to the salesman and tell him the deal was off. How embarrassing it was at the bank. How humiliating to walk out of that bank knowing that they knew I had egg all over my face. The testimony I was hoping to leave with the bankers had vanished with the Christian farmer's call to them.

As we neared the dealership, I tried to think the best of the Christian farmer. I reasoned: *Maybe, just maybe, there had been a mistake. Surely, he would call the salesman, the bankers and us and get it all straightened out.* That thinking would prove to be futile.

We drove into the dealership lot and nearly ran into the office. I asked one of the employees if they could get the salesman who had sold us the car. The employee seemed extremely surprised to see us again and went to find our salesman, who approached us with a surprised look also on his face. "What's the problem? Why are you back?" he asked. I struggled to get the words out as I said that there must have been a mistake, and then continued to tell him about our visit to the bank and the phone call from our mutual friend to the loan manger. When I told him what the farmer had said in the call, the salesman's look of disbelief was obvious. "What? That is impossible! He clearly told me that he would purchase the car of your choice!" he exclaimed. Now the salesman was as confused as we were.

"Are you absolutely sure that is what he told you?" I asked him.

"Yes!" He answered, sounding somewhat annoyed.

At that point, I apologized and asked him if we could simply cancel the whole thing and exchange the automobiles? The look on

IN THE WAR

his face sent shivers through me. He said, "I'm afraid it's not going to be that simple. I've already sold your car to another dealer in the city." I looked at him with utter surprise and an obvious look of fear. I was getting nauseated as I stood there, dumbfounded, when he continued, "This is unbelievable. Are you sure you can't simply take out a loan to cover the difference yourself?"

I answered, "I'm sorry sir, but I simply can't afford a loan. I am sorry."

Again, he said, "This is totally unbelievable, but I will see what I can do to get your car back before it's sold again." As he walked away, I knew he was very annoyed and angry with me, the Christian farmer, and undoubtedly, the whole situation. I just wanted to disappear.

We stood in the dealership for over an hour, waiting and praying that the salesman could retrieve our old car. It was extremely hard on Trudy and the girls. They were as tired and embarrassed as I was. Every now and then the men in the dealership would glance over at us with what seemed to be an odd look on their faces. A look that said, 'I can't believe there are people like that.' It was a very humiliating and uncomfortable situation to be in.

Finally, the salesman approached us and said, "Well I was able to get your old car back. They are bringing it over right now." I was so relieved, but anger was also welling up more and more. The car arrived, and we tore up the check and the sales agreement. We took the licence plates from the new car that we were returning and placed them back on our old car. I apologized to the salesman, and we began the journey back home, exhausted, and humiliated.

We arrived home rather late and went to bed, confused, and extremely disappointed. The time and money we had spent going to Saskatoon and back was a loss. I was feeling like I had been used and abused. I could not help but think of the poor witness the whole thing was to our bankers and the dealership in Saskatoon. A feeling of anger and resentment seemed to be settling in my gut. I felt so bad that my girls had to witness this sort of thing. How could I get myself into this mess?

The telephone rang rather early the next morning. Trudy answered and on the other end was the Christian farmer. He asked if I was at home. Trudy answered, "Yes, but he doesn't want to talk to you right now."

"Oh," he said, "What's wrong?"

Trudy boldly replied, "You lied to us!"

His answer was sharp and filled with anger, "No, it was a test!"

"Don't you ever play God in our lives again," Trudy responded.

At this point, the farmer became terribly angry and started shouting over the telephone at my wife. "You can't talk to me like that! You are a woman, and women are not to talk to men like that! I'm going to have you guys kicked out of your town and out of the ministry."

Once again Trudy said, "You lied to us and don't you ever play God in our lives again!"

"Have Bob call me later," he shouted, and then hung up.

When Trudy told me about the conversation, I was devastated. I really did not want to believe it. He deceived us to test us. Test us for what? I felt like the proverbial rabbit that was led into the trap by following the carrot on the string.

We spent much time praying before I telephoned him the next day. He was extremely angry at me. I said, "You lied to us."

"I did not," was his response.

I continued, "You totally deceived us. You deceived us to test us."

He continued shouting and threatening to have me kicked out of the ministry. After a while he did admit that he had deceived us so he could test me to see if I was a greedy person. His final word to me was, "You should not be in ministry." Then he hung up on me. That was the last time we heard from the Christian farmer.

170

Chapter 23

OUR CHURCH WILL PAY FOR IT

Our evangelistic ministry was slowly becoming known as a ministry that God was using to reap many souls for Christ. In the late 1980s and early 1990s we were conducting a lot of North American crusades. Many of these evangelistic campaigns were held in small rural towns on the prairies of Canada. At the time, it was my privilege to have a talented and popular musical family, as well as a talented pianist, touring with me as part of my team. This ministry of music was indeed a crowd pleaser and was used of God to help draw an audience. It was also evident that their music was used by the Lord to prepare the hearts of the listening audience for the message of repentance and salvation.

One cold winter month, (not uncommon on the prairies), we were conducting one such crusade in yet another small, out-of-the-way town. The week-long crusade was received well by the small town and was a great success. The pastor and his congregation were overjoyed at the response of over seventy people, who came forward in repentance and received Christ as their Lord and Savior.

Following the crusade, Trudy and I spent an afternoon with the pastor and his wife and family. We enjoyed a nice dinner and warm fellowship together while our conversation centered on the

BOB MCLAUGHLIN

success of the crusade and our ministries in general. We had a good time in praise and prayer, thanking the Lord for His intervention in the lives of so many people in their small town.

Eventually, the pastor voiced a concern he had. He said he felt that I should be driving a more reliable vehicle. At this point I feel it is imperative for our readers to understand that neither my wife nor I made any mention of our need for a newer vehicle to them or to anyone during the entire campaign. I was extremely reluctant to discuss his concern further with regards to this subject as we were still stinging from the previous experience with the Christian farmer. The more he persisted, the more uncomfortable I became.

He told us that he used to be a car salesman and would love to recommend several dealerships and friends who could help us select a good car. I told him we were not in the market for buying a newer car, and furthermore, we were not in a financial position to do so. His immediate response was "I know that our church would be more than willing to cover the payments. Your ministry here in our town was probably the most effective evangelistic campaign this town has ever experienced." He continued, "And furthermore, my wife and I will contribute fifty dollars a month toward the payments ourselves." I said that we were grateful that they would be so kind, but we really were not in the market for a newer car. Unfortunately, he continued to turn up the heat by implying that I was placing my family in harm's way each time I put them in our little car. This accusation hurt. and I said a silent prayer asking God to help me deal with this situation.

At this point, I felt it was necessary to give him a little insight into our experience with the Christian farmer. Without disclosing names, I shared with him the very painful story. They sat there in total astonishment as I unfolded the story. When I had finished sharing, they could hardly believe that a Christian would do such a thing. We assured them that every detail was indeed true and that we were still recovering from the ordeal, and therefore we were not

IN THE WAR

in any way desiring to purchase another vehicle at this time. Surely, now they would understand and drop the subject, but they were determined to pursue the issue. The pastor responded, "We believe with all our hearts that we have been brought into your lives to be used by God to get you folks a more reliable car." He continued to assure us that the church would make up the difference needed, along with their $50 a month, to pay for the car. He would bring it up to the church leaders at the next leadership meeting and be in touch with us regarding the outcome. In closing he said, "Let's see what will come of this." All we could do was repeat that we were thankful but not interested.

After a few days I received a call from the pastor and he said that he had spoken with a friend of his, an auto dealer, and this friend had the perfect car for us. He went ahead and made the arrangements for me to meet with him and test drive the car. I was reluctant but went along with the idea. That car proved to be a lemon; and thankfully we were able to avoid that one. Yet this pastor was persistent and refused to let this go.

A day or two later the pastor found another car for about $3,000 and assured me this was not only an incredibly good deal but also an incredibly good car. He told me to take out a loan for the full amount and that he and the church would make the monthly payments. I was in a dilemma. I realized that we were not going to avoid this situation, so against my better judgement, we yielded, thinking that it could not happen again. Surely these people were fully willing to make the payments for us. So, I cautiously, yet optimistically, fully trusted them to do as they said they would.

The monthly payments turned out to be $130 per month for the next three years. I telephoned the pastor and informed him of the amount and again he assured me I would start receiving a monthly check for $130.00. The first check to arrive from the church was for $50.00. The following checks that arrived were for the same

173

amount. That sick feeling in the pit of my stomach returned and I thought, *Oh no, not again!*

We struggled to scratch together the remaining $80.00 per month needed to make the payments. I decided that I should call the pastor and inquire as to what was going on. When I phoned him, he simply told me that the church had agreed to send only $50.00 per month. He assured me the difference would be made up soon. The amount never changed; however, something did change after only a few months when I received a stinging letter from the church leadership. They insisted that they wanted more detail as to how the $50 per month was being spent. At that point I began to believe that the pastor never talked with them regarding the money being used to buy a car. The church had been receiving our newsletters the same as all other supporters on our mailing list and they detailed our ministry travels as well as the results. These reports were always filled with thanks for their support and clearly explained where the donations were being used.

When I realized that the pastor had not explained the car situation, I wasn't sure what I should do. But then I felt that it was best to let the pastor deal with it.

The next month I received a letter from the same church informing us that they were dropping their support of $50 per month. I never heard from the pastor again. He never apologized or sent an explanation, and he never sent the $50 per month he had personally pledged to us for the car. In short, he dropped totally out of our lives, and we were left with another car we really did not want, along with a $130 monthly payment we really could not afford. We made those payments out of our own pocket for the next two years. So, sadly, we were forced to give up on that kind and persistent comment of "Our church will pay for it."

Chapter 24

IF YOU EVER HAVE A NEED

How many times have you heard someone say, "If you ever have a need just let us know?" Or how many times have we said the same thing with good intentions, meaning every word with all our heart? Or so we thought at the time we said it. For many of us we are willing to admit we have been guilty of making a statement like that rather glibly or tritely. At the time it seemed it was just the thing to say, so we said it. Usually, we blurt it out following some misfortune we have become aware of that has befallen a friend, loved one or an acquaintance. However, those of us who are children of God should know better and should carefully guard against making these statements lightly. Yet, somehow, we too can find ourselves making the mistake often.

For those of us in the ministry, especially those of us in ministries that are on the receiving end of Christian generosity and totally dependent on financial donations from those who make up the body of Christ, we tend to understand that if a Christian makes this kind of statement, he is fully aware that it usually means one of two things. First, and foremost he should expect that he or she might receive a request for prayer. Second, he should not be surprised to receive a request for financial assistance.

Prayer seems to be the most common offer from the Christian overall. This is only good when the person offering to pray for our needs is truly willing to follow through with his offer. Of course, when it comes to prayer one can never know if those who offer to pray really do pray. Based on personal experience the majority may offer but sadly fail to follow through. I stress here that this is not true of all. Some follow through and pray for the individuals needs as promised.

When it comes to determining if the person is following through as he promised there is no way of truly knowing. There is nothing to measure with. Here some would argue that if our needs were met, then that is evidence of their faithfulness to do as promised. This is not always true. If you have fifty people who promise to pray for your needs and your needs are met, this does not prove that all fifty were praying as promised. God may have answered the prayers of only one person because the other forty-nine did not pray as promised. Perhaps all fifty did not pray as promised and God answered our own prayers. God can do whatever He pleases and meet the need with or without prayer.

So, with all this in mind it's easy to see and understand why many offer to pray. Simply put, there is no visible component by which to measure human accountability so to speak. Often our humanity chooses the easier way. This side of heaven who would know.

However, when it comes to money there is an automatic, built in, visible accountability factor. Of course, that will be seen when the gift has been delivered as promised. If the money shows up, they were faithful to come through with their promise. If the money does not show up, well, they were not faithful to their promise, and they also know that you know they were not faithful.

In the many years of depending on God to meet our needs through Christian people we have seen many faithful to their

IN THE WAR

promises to send in their financial gifts. However, over the years we have seen as many, if not more, fail to come through with their promises.

Over the years of active ministry, we have noticed when a financial investor stops sending their support there seems to be a similar attitude that inevitably prevails among them. Our human nature tends to force us to justify the reason for discontinuing a financial promise. So as not to feel guilty once they do break their promise to God and the individual they support, they usually convince themselves that there is something to their disliking about the church, pastor, missionary, or evangelist. If the truth be known, (and it will be some day) they usually just want the money to use elsewhere for their own selfish pleasures. Commitment simply flies away.

I am always amazed at the shallow commitments some Christians make to the Lord, especially when it comes to money they have promised to give. I had one man who made a $5 per month pledge, who said to me while I was giving him a report on our ministry, "You're the first one I cut when I can't meet my budget." The $5 per month commitment he made should have been thought through prior to making that commitment. What was I to say in response to this remark? It did clarify the reason we were not receiving it. He never sent us another donation. Another couple who had made a $20 per month commitment stopped sending their donations as well. When we returned to their area to give a report, we met with them and a few other people at a mutual friends' home. I remember vividly that night as I was giving my report. The one who had stopped sending his $20 leaned over with a smirk on his face and taking my suit jacket sleeve between his fingers and rubbing the material together he said, "It sure must be nice to be an evangelist." The obvious implication being that if you are an evangelist, you can afford nice clothes. The suit was the only suit I owned. I was embarrassed and hurt but said nothing. I looked around the room and everyone was smiling in agreement.

177

Not one came to our rescue. They never sent the ministry any more donations. To make matters worse, the others who were present that night also stopped sending their donations as well.

What really hurt was the fact that these people had all been baptized together with us. They were all in our weekly Bible study group for three years prior to our going in the ministry. What had happened? Why were they cutting their support? Was it jealousy? To this day we have never been able to understand why all of them seemed to turn against us and the ministry we were involved in. Each time we were in their area we always attempted to restore those dear friendships, but they made it clear to us that they did not care to fellowship with us. This broke our hearts.

Another incident took place many years ago and was the reason for the name of this chapter. We had made an acquaintance with a young couple who had a business near our town. The business was a father and sons farming business which produced various farm equipment. It was remarkably successful.

The young couple had been sponsoring our ministry financially on a frequent basis. I remember he said to me one day, "If you ever have a need, let us know." I remember how serious he was when he said it to me. In fact, he even went so far as to say, "Bob, I'm serious about this. If you ever have a need, come to me." Well, it was not long before a serious need developed, and I was on the telephone with him. I told him that I would not have phoned him had he not been so insistent about sharing our needs with them. I shared with him of what we were looking for. I challenged him to help meet this necessity. He asked how much was required to reach our goal. So, I told him how much it would be. He said he wanted to discuss it with his wife and would call us back in a few minutes. He called me back a few minutes later and invited us over for dinner the following weekend. The appointment came and we had a great time enjoying good food and warm fellowship. That was about to change rather abruptly. While Trudy and his wife did the dishes, he

IN THE WAR

asked me to put my coat on and follow him out to the barn/wood-shed. Once we were in the barn, he turned to me and handed me a check for the full amount I had challenged him with. However, the look on his face was telling and giving off vibes that I knew would produce some rather unpleasant comments. I was shocked at the comments he made to me. He said rather sternly, "Don't ever do this again!" I asked him, "What do you mean?" He answered rather firmly and loud, "Just what I said, don't ever do this again!" At this point the joy of receiving his donation was fading quickly. The look of total confusion on my face must have prompted him to enlighten me. He said, "Bob, if you had a need that God wanted me to meet, He would have told me through the Holy Spirit!" I answered him saying; "You told me that if I ever had a need that I was to contact you." Frustrated and confused, I offered to give back the check at that point. He declined and simply told me to never do this again. I complied and never did it again.

After that evening, we did on occasion receive some more dona-tions from them for the ministry. With each of these donations we would always send an appropriate thank you but eventually they stopped sending financial donations. The lesson for us has been to be very careful to tell someone to contact us saying, "If you ever have a need."

Chapter 25

I WILL SEE TO IT YOU NEVER STEP FOOT IN THIS PULPIT AGAIN!

While flying home over the Atlantic Ocean following an intense and fruitful evangelistic campaign in the former Soviet Union, I was reminded that I was to preach in a chapel service at a Bible college the day after I got home. In those early days of ministry this was not uncommon for my schedule.

I do remember having a bit of concern doing this chapel service because just the week before a very prominent international youth speaker had just completed a huge nation-wide youth rally held at this same college.

It was common knowledge that this speaker was paid a rather handsome sum to come to this event. He was picked up at the airport and driven back to the airport in the college vehicle used only for top administrators and for the VIPs who graced that campus.

I did not have a clue what I was to preach on and, as a habit, I enquired of the Lord for a message from Him.

I arrived at the airport and was met by my lovely wife and children. We collected my belongings and began our drive home, stopping in a small city for pizza. This was our common family practice upon my return from a major trip overseas.

BOB MCLAUGHLIN

That night I had a peace before going to bed that the Lord would give me the message in the morning before the service. This too was often how the Lord worked in our ministry.

Morning came, and God gave me the perfect message which I preached with unusual authority and power. A simple straight forward message of repentance. When I gave the invitation to repent and come forward well over 200 students came forward, many in tears. Following the message my practice was to vacate the premises as soon as possible and get alone with the Lord, which I did, leaving the follow-up to the staff.

I found out later that one of the college professors who attended that chapel service, upon seeing what God was doing, ran to the administration office and requested help in counselling those who came forward. Many of the administrators left their desks and made their way to the service.

I also found out later that the classes immediately following the chapel service were either cancelled or began very late because of the unusual moving of God on the student body. We heard later that the Vice President of the College called that meeting a "mini revival."

However, not all staff and faculty in the college appreciated that service, and especially the ending of the service. In fact, some were extremely upset that class schedules were disturbed. They voiced their disapproval to the leadership.

One faculty member called me and told me in no uncertain terms that I did not have the authority to do what I did. When I questioned him further, he reminded me of a statement I made while giving the invitation. What he was referring to was that I had said, "I will take full responsibility if you are late for class! Don't leave without dealing with the sin God has put His finger on this morning." He stressed that I did not have that kind of authority because I was not a faculty or staff member. I responded truthfully saying that God gave me the authority, and that I would have

IN THE WAR

disobeyed Him had I not handled the ending of the service the way He desired. He did not agree with me.

As a preacher of God's Word, there have been several valuable lessons learned over the years. If God gives the message and fills the preacher with His power and His anointing, He can also stop the message in the timeframe He desires. His timing can and often does differ from man's. A preacher would do well to understand he should never yield to man but always obey God no matter how severe the consequences may be.

On several occasions prior to a given service and while meeting with church leadership for prayer, there would be a well-meaning pastor or elder/deacon who would request/suggest that I be sure to mention certain issues in the message, issues they felt the listening audience needed to hear. However, over the years I have discovered if I yielded to someone other than the Holy Spirit, and thus deviating from the God-given message for me to preach, the results were not good. Why? Because yielding to man rather than God is disobedience to God. Obedience to God is what God expects of His children, especially preachers.

A few months later I was asked to take a Sunday morning service at the same college. In those days, most campus residents attended Sunday services on campus. There was no pastor, so often staff and faculty and guests were invited to bring the message to campus residents and students alike. I began preparing a message that I thought would be appropriate, but it was not the one God was nudging me to preach. The battle was on. To my shame admittedly it was the comment I had received from the faculty member after the last message I preached on campus that was influential in my current preparation. I was afraid to preach what God wanted because I knew there would be serious consequences.

As the Sunday approached, God's conviction was heavy on me to preach His message. I fought it. Truthfully, I was hoping He would allow me to preach the message I was preparing but His

183

Spirit would not ease up and the battle intensified throughout the entire Saturday night before I was to preach.

The service began and sitting on the platform the battle intensified with each passing moment. I prayed, almost begging the Lord to allow me to preach my message but to no avail. Before long I was being introduced and between the chair I was sitting in and the pulpit I finally surrendered and preached God's message.

It really was a very simple message, and when I gave the invitation, over one hundred came forward to repent. It was an amazing service as God's Holy Spirit fell upon those dear people.

As was my usual habit, I vacated the premises as soon as those who came forward were being dealt with.

About five days later I received a telephone call from one of the staff asking if he could meet with me in a day or two. We set a date and arranged the meeting.

After all the niceties he said, "Bob, every time you preach here God does amazing things." He went on to say "however, there were a couple of things that weren`t appreciated." "They", meaning leadership, were not pleased with the time I took in the previous chapel service which interrupted with the regular scheduled class time. Now, it was a certain comment I had made in the Sunday morning message. I had made a rather bold comment during that morning`s message. He quoted me saying, "there is sin in the hallways of administration." I remember that was one of the reasons I struggled with the Lord about that message. Before leaving his office he strongly suggested I "be careful with comments like that."

A few weeks later I was having lunch with an influential faculty member of the same Bible college and the same issue came up. I remained adamant that God had given me the message and that what I had said was from Him and not from me. He sharply disagreed and commented that when someone is a guest preacher, they usually say nice things about the institute. He was pushing for an apology. I refused to apologize for preaching what God wanted

IN THE WAR

me to preach. I even told him how I had struggled with the Lord the whole night before about that message and yet God insisted I preach His message. I told him I had to obey the Lord to which he suggested the message was not from the Lord but from myself. I stood firm and remained adamant.

At this point he began to shout, "When you stand in that pulpit you would do well to remember that pulpit belongs to this institute!" I said, "there's your problem sir, that pulpit belongs to God!" He began stabbing the end of his finger on the table and shouted, "I will see to it you never preach in this pulpit again unless you promise to only say nice things about this institute." I refused. At this point I was becoming disturbed by all that was unfolding, and it came out in my next comment. I raised my voice and said, "I refuse to lick your boots!" It was years before I was ever allowed to preach there again.

Now here is the amazing truth about the message God led me to preach that day and the comment that caused so much irritation from the leadership.

Several years later a very sad truth was exposed. It was discovered that there was indeed sin in the halls of administration. These sins, which will remain unnamed, were taking place at the time when the Lord led me to preach that message. Though these sad sinful events were swept under the rug so to speak, and I was accused of preaching a message that was not from God, God made it clear that He was the one who from the pulpit that day said, "There is sin in the hallways of administration!" I was just his mouthpiece.

There can be negative consequences and often are for the preacher who preaches what God wants rather than what man wants. In this case, it was nine years before I was allowed back in that pulpit.

Some might ask, was it worth the hassle and the embarrassment experienced in a public restaurant the day he shouted at me that the message was not from God? I can honestly say that it was indeed worth it.

Chapter 26

DON'T YOU THINK FOR ONE MINUTE THAT YOU CAN JUST COME HERE TO BE BLESSED AND FED

By now my slide was becoming rather severe. I knew I was in desperate need of help. My prayers were seemingly going unanswered. I was sliding deeper and deeper into my secret sin. My anger and resentments were fuelling the root of bitterness and eating at my soul like a cancer.

I needed someone I could trust, someone who would keep things confidential regarding all I was going through. So, I began to test the waters. On several occasions, I had carefully begun to share some of my frustrations with acquaintances, hoping to find someone I could confide in and help keep me accountable. Sadly, each time I got to that point it would become obvious that I could not share details of my frustrations with the person I was meeting with.

Trudy and I determined we needed to find a new church where we could eventually join as members. We decided to check out one in a nearby city. After several Sundays, we found a church where the Word of God was preached. We began attending regularly and eventually over time the church asked us to consider becoming members.

One day I received a call from the pastor of this new church. He extended an invitation to join him for a lunch meeting. I accepted and we planned to meet. We enjoyed a nice lunch, and the fellowship was warm.

I shared with him my appreciation for his pulpit ministry. I also thanked him for his interest in us as a family. After a few minutes, he turned the discussion to our evangelistic ministry. He informed me that he was aware of our worldwide ministry. I assumed he had seen us on the popular Christian program "100 Huntley Street" or read an insert into "Decision Magazine" reporting on one of our evangelistic campaigns in Russia. As the conversation moved along, he said that he wondered what frustrations I experienced in a ministry like ours. When he noticed I was a bit hesitant he shared some of his own frustrations to set me at ease. He was persistent. He began to imply that he could be trusted and that he had a good listening ear. I thought of the verse in the Bible where it says, *"Iron sharpens iron..."* Proverbs 27:17

At this point I became cautiously optimistic. I said, "Pastor our type of ministry is a very tiring ministry with many frustrations." He asked, "like what?" I continued, "I am in need of your kind of preaching. I need to be ministered too when I am not ministering. The campaigns I conduct all over the world are beginning to weigh heavy on me. I fear I may be in danger of heading into burnout." I continued to explain other concerns and frustrations. Eventually I said, "I need your help." He asked, "so, how do you think I can help you."

I took a deep breath and said, "ok, what I need is your permission and understanding to allow me the opportunity to recoup after each campaign." I continued, "Pastor, I need a church where I can come and be ministered to. A church where I can be blessed and fed in between these international campaigns." I continued, "as

IN THE WAR

much as I would like to get involved with teaching Sunday school or ushering, I just can't do it now. Perhaps over time we can be active in these kind of church activities, but for now I just need a church that will help me and feed me." He responded and said, "Well, let's see if I can help you." Following our meeting as I was driving home, I wondered how this would eventually turn out. As I mentioned earlier, I was cautiously optimistic.

The very next Sunday, our family drove to our new church. We were warmly greeted by church folk, and we took our seats together in a pew. I was looking forward to the pastor's message.

The service was shaping up to be a blessing as we sang hymns and opened in prayer. The pastor walked to the pulpit and after some opening remarks and other announcements he began his message. His message was good until he made the following statement. I remember seeing his arm extend outward and over the pulpit and with his index finger pointed directly at me and my family he shouted, "Don't you think for one minute that you can just come here and be blessed and fed!" My jaw dropped and I stared in disbelief at him. As our eyes locked, he almost squinted and slightly nodded displaying a look of (I mean what I say) before moving on in his message. I looked over at Trudy and she had that look of oh no not again. She squeezed my hand and said, "It's ok dear."

I was oblivious of the rest of his message. I totally shut down. Once the sermon was over and during the closing hymn, we got up and left the church before the benediction. I knew I was in no condition to talk with the pastor after his scathing remarks clearly directed at me from the pulpit. I was more than angry; I was livid.

My mind was racing with numerous thoughts. The one thought that kept coming back to me was a nagging question, "Why did he not tell me this during our lunch meeting less than 48 hours ago? We could have agreed to disagree and gone our separate ways. There was no good reason to express his opinion from the pulpit with regards to my sincere request. He may as well have thrown a

189

BOB MCLAUGHLIN

javelin through my already damaged heart." We took the hint and never returned to that church. No one from that church sought to find out why we never came back.

Sadly, my trust level towards the church in general and their pastors was rapidly declining to an all time low. I felt I could trust no one. I was seemingly adrift on a stormy sea without a rudder. The spiritual battle was intensifying with each passing day. My self pity was reaching an all time low as well. I knew I was destined for a painful future, and it was approaching quickly. Once again, to my great shame, I turned more and more to indulging in my secret sin.

Try as I may I was losing the battle. From this point on, whenever I would attempt to recoup and attend church services in between campaigns, inevitably the devil would shout in my ears, "Don't you think for one moment that you can just come here and be blessed and fed."

Chapter 27

NOW WE REALLY HAVE SOMETHING VERY EXCITING TO SHARE WITH YOU

I had recently returned from an extraordinarily successful evangelistic campaign in India. After taking a few days to get over jetlag and taking care of various administrative duties, we began our long drive to the West Coast. As usual, we had planned to give reports in churches and small groups of supporters and friends.

One of these churches had been supporting our ministry for a few years, and we had always enjoyed visiting this church and the many friends we had made over the years.

As is the case in many churches when a pastor steps down and a new one takes his place, the opinion of the new pastor often doesn't reflect the opinion of the previous pastor in regard to supported individuals like us. Such was the case in this church.

We sensed early on that this new pastor was not in favor of mass evangelism like ours. As always, we tried to maintain a warm relationship with all pastors, and we attempted the same with this man as well. Unfortunately, no matter what we did he would display his disapproval in unique ways.

The last time we were at this same church to give a report was the year before. As was our habit we contacted the pastor several weeks before coming out west. Together on the telephone we agreed on a Sunday morning for me to give a report. He told me on the phone that this allows him ample weeks to prepare the congregation by announcing our upcoming visit. He further said that he would spread the word to all the Bible study groups and each Sunday he would announce the date of our coming.

When we arrived in the church parking lot that scheduled Sunday we were in for a big surprise. As we were getting out of our vehicle, the chairman of the mission's department pulled in beside our car. As he was exiting his vehicle, I could see the confusion on his contorted face when he asked, "Oh my, this is a surprise, what are you guys doing here?" My heart sank. I asked him, "Did you not know of our coming to give report today?" He said, "No." I questioned further with, "So, you haven't heard the announcements of our coming in your services these last few weeks?" He said, "There have been no announcements of you guys coming." I told him his pastor promised to prepare the congregation with announcements each Sunday. He answered, "Well Bob, there have been no announcements of your coming." He continued, "No one knows you are here today."

We entered the church foyer and sure enough, everyone asked what we were doing there unannounced. The tone implied it was inappropriate to show up unannounced.

It became a very awkward service. The pastor said from the pulpit that Bob has requested people remain behind following the service so he can give you all his report. He said again, "That is Bob's request. This is what he prefers."

However, once he said that he followed it with this. "As you all know we have a family facing a difficult future, so I am requesting that after the service you all take time to meet with them in the foyer. Please take all the time you need to make sure this family knows that we as a congregation love them and stand in prayer with them through these difficult days." There was no mention that

IN THE WAR

there had been an agreement between us for him to prepare them for our coming weeks in advance.

It was obvious to me and Trudy that our reporting had been craftly sabotaged. Very few people came to our reporting time.

Later I made it a point to meet with the pastor and question him as to why this happened. His response was that I had failed to remind him of our agreement. That is right, it was all my fault. He said, "The next time we agree on a date, you are to remind me to write it in my schedule."

So that was the previous year. This time I had made sure the congregation was prepared for our scheduled reporting with notes and emails etc. However, we were in for another surprise displaying the pastor's disapproval of our ministry.

The Sunday morning arrived, and we drove to the church. We were excited to give a public report from the pulpit. We arrived early and met with the pastor for prayer before entering the formal service. When it came time for me to give the report, the pastor introduced me this way. He said in a rather disturbing way, even almost sighing, "Well, Bob and Trudy are back again and want to give a report." At that he motioned for me to come up on the platform and take the pulpit.

I bounded up onto the platform and thanked the pastor and greeted the congregation, thanking them for their support and prayers. I said, "We have some very exciting news to share with you regarding our recent campaign in India." I gave the report in detail and ended with excitement stating that in all the evangelistic meetings we conducted during this campaign we were privileged to witness over 10,000 public decisions for Christ. I looked at the people expecting a favorable response. I had hoped for an amen or praise the Lord. The silence of the congregation was deafening. But the worst was the rather blank expressions on some faces of the people. It seemed a bit icy to say the least. I thought to myself, "Why would they not be excited about so many people coming to Jesus?

BOB MCLAUGHLIN

What does it take to get them excited?" I was at a loss for an answer. Unknown to us we were about to find out what excites them. Once again, I thanked the pastor and the congregation for the time, they allowed me to share, and I vacated the platform and took my seat in the pew beside my wife and children. Trudy took my hand and whispered, "it's okay dear." She too could sense the cold response.

What happened next should cause every Christian to be sincerely concerned.

As I took my seat the pastor stood up and said, "Well, okay now we have something really exciting to share with you." I thought to myself, "What could possibly be more exciting than thousands of people coming to Jesus." Anyway, I thought well perhaps someone witnessed more than 10,000 decisions for Christ and will be giving their report. That indeed would be more exciting. I was in for the surprise of a lifetime.

The pastor called a young man up on the platform and to our great surprise he shared the following. The young man stood behind the pulpit and said, "God allowed me to win two round trip flight tickets to Hawaii." He continued, "but I decided to give them to my parents as an anniversary gift." To our great surprise the congregation burst forth with a thunderous applause and some gave a standing ovation!

We were stunned and frankly very disappointed. This response clearly revealed something tragically wrong with many North American churches.

The pastor stood grinning and applauding with glee over the response to the young man's report...and we believe he had orchestrated this with evil intent to assure us of his ongoing disapproval of our ministry.

Sadly, once again I fostered anger towards another person and pushed that anger deep inside my soul. My slide into developing a serious root of bitterness was becoming more intense. I was failing in the forgiveness department. I knew the enemy was having a hay day with me. Yet along with my festering resentments I was yielding more and more to my craving and found myself indulging in my secret sin even more and hating with a passion the words, "Now we really have something very exciting to share with you."

Preaching in India

PART SIX

THE CRUCIBLE YEARS AND REPENTANCE

Chapter 28

THE STORM APPROACHES

The blistering African noon-time sun was directly overhead in the crystal-clear blue sky. Its scorching heat beat down mercilessly on all who could not find shade. The large crowd had gathered for a lunch-hour meeting in the city park. We were conducting the last meeting of a three-week evangelistic campaign in and around the city of Eldoret, Kenya, Africa. The date was June 10, 2000.

Once the music stopped and the crowd had gathered, my wife Trudy, with the help of an excellent interpreter, gave her personal testimony to the attentive audience. Next, our interpreter introduced me, and I took my place along with him on the platform. Because of his perfect interpretation in Swahili, I was able to preach the life-changing message of the gospel. This meeting was not unlike hundreds of meetings that we had conducted all over the world in the last few years. However, this one would indeed prove to be unlike any of the previous meetings.

When I extended the invitation to repent and come forward to receive Christ, I stood there, as always, amazed at the sight unfolding before my eyes. Several hundred men, women, and children humbly came forward. To this day, I can still see their faces in my mind's eye. Many had sweat mingled with tears running down their beautiful faces as they stood in the blazing sun and prayed to receive Jesus as their Lord and Savior. Once I finished praying with them, I stepped off the platform and joined my wife in the shade of a nearby tree. I prayed a silent prayer of thanksgiving for yet another glorious harvest for the Kingdom of God.

As I looked over the crowd, I choked back tears of unworthiness and great shame because of my secret life. I wondered how long God was going to allow me to minister for Him. Guilt and shame washed over me again and again as I reminded myself that I was so unworthy of this privilege. I knew that God knew every detail of the double life that I was leading, yet for reasons known only to Him, He was still using me to preach the gospel to tens of thousands of lost souls all over the world. I knew that eventually a time would come when God would deal with my sin. After all, how many times had I preached on the need to repent of sin? How many times had I shouted from the platform the passage of Scripture taken from Galatians 6:7-8 which says, *"Do not be deceived, God is not mocked; for whatever a man sows, this he will also reap. For the one who sows to his own flesh will from the flesh reap corruption, but the one who sows to the Spirit will from the Spirit reap eternal life."*? (NASB) How many times had I heard well-meaning Christians say, "God cannot use a dirty vessel"? My sinful life, while I continued to lead others to Christ, literally flew in the face of that kind of comment. But I was keenly aware of the passage in Numbers 32:23b, *"...be sure your sin will find you out."* (NASB) Also, the Gospel of Luke records a warning that Jesus gave His disciples: *"But there is nothing covered up that will not be revealed and hidden that will not be known."* (Luke 12:2 NASB)

So yes, I knew that eventually the day would come when God would deal with my hidden sin. However, I had no idea that the evangelistic sermon I just gave would be the last sermon I would preach for many years to come. The dark storm clouds were gathering on the horizon for me. Harvest time had arrived for the secret seeds of sin I had sown.

IN THE WAR

We returned home from Africa following that amazingly successful evangelistic campaign. Thousands had surrendered to Jesus, and we were looking forward to completing three more evangelistic campaigns before the end of the year. So, we began preparing for our next ministry coming up in about three weeks. We put out our newsletter to our supporting constituents, thanked them for their support and announced the upcoming campaign. We requested prayer and mentioned the need for finances to cover flight tickets and in-country expenses. For years we had operated this exact way and God had always met our needs. Often the finances we required arrived just a day or two before departure and I simply assumed this one would be no different. I could not have been more wrong. Simply put, we were astonished when not a single penny came in for the campaign. In fact, sadly, we were forced to cancel the entire campaign.

Though we were disappointed, I attempted to remain positive and began to focus on the last two international campaigns we had planned for the year 2000. I prayed much but kept sinning in secret. I sent out faxes, emails, and newsletters explaining the need for resources to conduct these important international campaigns but all to no avail. Every campaign for the rest of 2000 had to be cancelled. It was then that I realized God had withdrawn His provision and I was reaping the severe consequences of my willful and deliberate act of disobedience and sin. What I did not know was that this was only the beginning of God's loving discipline.

Preaching in Eldoret, Kenya

Preaching in Africa

IN THE WAR

Preaching in Africa

Preaching in Africa

Chapter 29

A SECRET SIN EXPOSED

It was now early December of 2000. Trudy would go out the door for work just before eight in the morning and I would sit in my office drinking wine, my heart full of fear until the wine would take effect. I knew that my deliberate sin was now beginning to reap the consequences. I cried out daily to God, asking for His forgiveness. In doing so, I was hoping my sin would remain secret and out of people's sight. Nearly every time I prayed that request, it seemed God would remind me of a verse of scripture I had often quoted: *"Do not be deceived, God is not mocked; for whatever a man sows, this he will also reap. For the one who sows to his own flesh will from the flesh reap corruption, but the one who sows to the Spirit will from the Spirit reap eternal life."* (Galatians 6:7-8 NASB)

The truth is, I was guilty, and God had had enough! My secret sin of alcoholism began ten years earlier on November 4, 1990, while preaching in the First Baptist Church of Moscow, Russia. As mentioned in a previous chapter, I had not consumed alcohol for seventeen and a half years when I was faced with the communion service where real wine was used. That was the beginning of the end which now was quickly approaching.

During those ten years I developed the habit of consuming alcohol on nearly all my flights. On international flights, I was often so intoxicated upon arrival at my destination that, when I awoke from my drunken stupor, I seldom knew what country I was in.

To keep this sin of drunkenness a secret from my national team, I booked flights that arrived at least a day or two in advance to allow me time to sober up before meeting any nationals. As I lay severely hungover in bed in my hotel room, the fog lifting from my aching brain, I would realize where I was and why I was in that country. Tears would fill my eyes and I would fall on my face before the Lord and weep over my blatant sin. Each time this happened, I vowed to the Lord that this was the last time and that I was going to quit drinking altogether. I would beg God to not allow my sin to interfere with the campaign. Amazingly, and for reasons known only to God, He would answer my prayer. The campaigns would last more than two weeks and were a tremendous success as thousands would surrender their lives to Jesus.

I never consumed alcohol during my campaigns. This added to my ability to claim that I was not an alcoholic. It is commonly thought that a real alcoholic can't go a day without a drink. How wrong that is. At the end of each campaign, after I had said goodbye to my team members, I would board my international flight home. Because I was a frequent flyer and was often bumped up to business class, my champagne glass would always be full. Each time I sat in that plane, my promise to God would quickly evaporate, I would push my feelings of guilt aside and proceed to get drunk.

For the most part I was able to sober up before arriving back home. Over the years, Trudy suspected I was leading a double life and yet hoped it wasn't true. Surely her husband, a preacher of the gospel, would not lie to her – would he? Eventually I was unable to hide the smell of stale alcohol oozing from my pores when I arrived at my home airport. Trudy would confront me, and I would lie time and time again.

Trudy was persistent and eventually I confessed only that I was having wine with my meals on flights. I used the excuse that the

IN THE WAR

alcohol helped me to sleep on the long flights. Trudy would raise her disapproval and I would defend myself insisting that I could drink socially now and that I was no longer an alcoholic. Then I would point out that many doctors approve of consuming wine for health reasons. Some doctors even suggest that having a couple glasses of wine a day is good for the body. I would even quote scripture in my defense.

Though Trudy was not convinced, she gave in to me and I craftily convinced her that we could have wine on special occasions with our dinner. Of course, I could think of all kinds of reasons to have a special occasion. I even convinced her to join me in drinking wine with our daily meals. Sadly, this went on for years and now, here we were in December of 2000. All my campaigns, starting in July, had been cancelled. My drinking amounted to my being drunk nearly every day. Many days, Trudy would come home from work only to be met by a drunken husband. This often turned into a sad confrontation and each morning I would beg her forgiveness, after she informed me of my actions the night before. She would graciously forgive me and beg me to seek help. I often responded with, "Honey, I can beat this with your help." Even today as I write these events, my heart still aches for all that I carelessly put my faithful and loving wife through.

December 6, 2000, dawned, and I continued with my daily alcohol consumption after Trudy left for work. During the day, I discovered that a Christmas event was planned that evening. Once I learned of this, I was determined to attend with Trudy. When she arrived home, I was dressed for the event but, as usual, I was drunk. She said, "What's the occasion?"

I responded, "I am taking my beautiful wife to a special event tonight; go and get ready."

Trudy said, "Honey, you are drunk! You really do not want to do this and everyone will know you are drunk. You can't hide it. Hon, please let's just stay home." Her pleas fell on drunken ears, and I demanded she get ready. I vaguely remember hearing something like, "OK sweetheart, I'm done trying to protect you and your ministry. I'll get ready and we will go. Whatever happens, will happen."

I remember some of what happened next, but mostly I have relied on the testimony of my wife and others. We walked through the doors of the event, and we removed our winter coats and hung them on the coat rack. When I turned around, an organizer of the event shook my hand and said, "Welcome here, Bob."

My response was something along the lines of, "You don't care about me." Sadly, I also swore at him.

He replied with, "Bob, put your coat on and go home." I uttered some unkind words and, we put on our coats and went home.

December 7, 2000, began with Trudy gently shaking my shoulder to wake me. My head was throbbing as I barked, "What do you want?"

She replied, "Someone just phoned, and he will call back in a few minutes. He wants to talk with you about last night."

I sat up and began trying to recapture the events of the previous evening. Trudy gave me some coffee and then went over everything that had happened. I sat in our living room with my head hanging down, realizing that this was most likely the end of my evangelistic preaching career.

The telephone rang and I was told, "Bob, you need to come to our office for a meeting."

"No, I don't. If you want to meet with me, you guys come to my office." I replied.

They said they would come later that morning. They arrived and sat down in our living room and one man began with, "Bob, you were drunk last night." He continued, "You have a drinking problem, but I think there's more than just the alcohol – am I right?"

I lied and said, "No, it's just a problem with alcohol." Anger filled my heart as I looked him in the eye. I could not believe that this man, who was sitting in the very chair he sat in a few weeks before

IN THE WAR

as we drank wine together, had now blown the whistle on me. I never exposed his alcohol consumption, which was against company policy.

Then, the other man said, "Bob, I'm going to allow you to confess to your board of directors. I will give you a couple of days. If I do not hear from your board chairman that you have confessed, I will personally expose your sin myself."

As I watched them leave our home, I wondered what would have happened if they had wrapped their arms around me and asked how they could help. Once the door had closed, I turned to Trudy and told her that this was the end of our ministry, and then I promptly got drunk

A day later I made one of the most difficult telephone calls I have ever made in my life. I called the chairman of our board of directors and told him everything and that I was going to resign from the ministry. He pleaded with me to not resign and that together we would seek help. I agreed to go into rehab, but I was still totally convinced that I was done with the ministry.

A day or so later I had a total mental meltdown and absolutely demolished my entire office. I was screaming and cursing as I smashed everything. I turned over my desk and chairs and threw my computer and printer across the room. There was glass everywhere. When I was finished, I collapsed in a heap. I was a totally broken man, sitting, and weeping in my demolished office. I thought I had finally hit bottom and just wanted to die. I checked myself into rehab and after twenty-eight days I came out sober. We shut down the ministry and I faithfully attended a 12-step program. Eventually, I secured a job with an airline, so we sold our home and moved to Alberta. At first, my work as a flight attendant was enjoyable. However, I found it difficult to attend the program while I was in the airline industry, and after only six months of sobriety, I was drunk again. I had yielded to the same lie all alcoholics wrestle with – I can now control my drinking. But I was wrong again!

209

Chapter 30

A PAINFUL SEPARATION

We had high hopes for a new beginning. We were now in a new city and my new job as a flight attendant with a Canadian airline was going well. Trudy had secured a job at a leisure travel company.

At this point, church was no longer a part of our lives. Sadly, I was so angry at the way we were treated and the loss of the ministry, that I turned my back on the church in general. I vowed I would never trust anyone again. It seemed apparent that many who had become our Christian friends over the years were not interested in finding us. Case in point: we received only two letters following our resignation from the ministry. One was semi encouraging, and the other was extremely harsh. My attitude was, after all those years and all those people, after traveling the world, including some exceedingly difficult areas, to preach the gospel – only two letters? Really? After ministering in dozens of churches across North America and after all the sacrifices we made as a family, it just didn't seem fair. I was having a huge pity party and I hated it all. I wanted to believe that I still loved the Lord, but I was in a terrible place in my relationship with Him. Deep in my heart, I blamed Him for everything. In public I would appear happy, for the most part, but I was a miserable man and deep in sin.

BOB MCLAUGHLIN

My flight attendant work was a good job, but it took me away from Trudy many nights each month. Those nights away were spent in hotels selected for crew members by the company. Initially I was working on 'milk runs,' which is what we called the short hops throughout the western part of Canada. The first year I worked 650 flights. Eventually, with the expansion of the company, we were conducting longer flights, both across the country and to sunny destinations during winter months.

Amazingly, I was able to remain sober – for a few months. However, the temptations were mounting and becoming more frequent. It became especially difficult during long layovers in far away cities. Though I knew and practiced the guidelines laid out in the 12-step program, I was becoming weak, and I knew it. My resentments increased, which is dangerous for an alcoholic. I began entertaining the classic alcoholic thought: *surely, I can have a drink and not lose control, like in the past. I know I can handle this drinking.* Sadly, I eventually yielded to those foolish thoughts.

I remember the night and place when I gave in. Our crew had worked several flights and we ended our day in Toronto, Ontario, where we would spend the night. After we checked into the hotel at the airport, I went straight to my room and called Trudy. I was tired and hungry, but I knew I had to call her before I did anything else. I was angry at myself for having to fight this battle to remain clean and sober, but to help me stay accountable we had arranged to talk on the telephone whenever possible. That night we had a good talk, but a plan was beginning to form in the back of my mind.

After our telephone conversation, I sat on my bed while an intense battle raged within me. I knew what I should do. I should call a member of Alcoholics Anonymous, and they would help me derail the strong desire to drink. I chose to not make that call. I also knew that for most alcoholics, the disease of alcoholism is like a sleeping lion, and it is a dangerous thing to disturb the lion.

212

I do believe that in some cases God will supernaturally deliver an individual from this disease. Why? Because He is God, and nothing is impossible for Him. However, most alcoholics do not see a miraculous delivery. Most addicts need to work through a 12-step program which is designed to help them maintain sobriety, one day at a time.

I was keenly aware of all of this, yet the battle was raging on inside of me, and the longer I fought it, the weaker I became. I knew I was playing with fire. Yet, sadly, I began giving into the temptation and became willing, once again, to risk everything and to place myself directly in the fire. Then it happened – I caved. I picked up the telephone, called room service and ordered a half-liter of wine. Within minutes it was delivered to my room. I lifted the first glass to my lips, and before taking a sip of the wine, I attempted to assure myself that I could control this thing, but I was wrong. Minutes later, as the half-liter of wine I had already polished off was taking effect, I was on the phone, once again, to order another half-liter. After only six months of sobriety, I was drunk again.

The next morning, I woke up and guilt washed over me. As the fog began to lift, I started to put pieces of the previous night together. When I saw the empty wine containers and wine glass, the terrible reality began to set in, and hit me hard, like a sledgehammer. *Oh no,* I thought, *I have failed one more time.* I was so enraged at myself, God, and everyone. Once again, I had broken my promise to myself and my wife – not to mention, my Lord.

I began to spiral out of control – again! Over the next few months, I continued to drink whenever legal time for drinking during layovers was allowed by the Federal Aviation Administration. Airlines have strict policies in place for alcohol consumption. I would arrange my flights so I'd have long layovers when I could feed my addiction during legal hours, with the hope that Trudy would never find out. This led to other sins, which often accompanied the drinking, and sent me spiralling even more out of control. For the most part, I was able to stay within the guidelines and policies of the airline, but my drinking and carousing was utterly disgraceful. I hated myself with an intense hatred.

It was not long before my dear wife Trudy suspected that I was drinking again and confronted me about it. Of course, I once again lied through my teeth. I knew she loved me, and I loved her, but I also knew that if she found out about my carousing and drinking, she would not put up with it anymore.

Several weeks passed before she confronted me again. I confessed that I had slipped a couple of times but that I was determined to beat my drinking problem. Trudy was devastated, so she did something many of us would not venture to do. Before going to sleep one night, she went to the Lord in brave, child-like faith, with a specific and detailed prayer request. She told the Lord that she was at her wit's end and did not know what to do and that she needed His clear direction. She told Him that, as she read through the Old Testament, she noted that He would often instruct people in what to do by giving them a dream. So, she asked God to give her a dream, detailing what He wanted her to do.

That very night God answered her prayer and gave her a vivid and extremely detailed dream. In the dream Trudy was directed to leave me but not to divorce me. She was told to go to our daughter's home in Saskatchewan and live with her. She was shown how she would have her own cleaning business and eventually her own home. She was not to worry about her future but to trust God with everything.

When she awoke, she knew exactly what she was to do, but she asked God if she could give her husband one more chance. If I continued to drink, she would do exactly what she was told to do in the dream. She specifically asked for one more month and God granted both of her requests.

Trudy told me she was giving me one more chance. "I'm giving you a full month," she said. "If you abstain from consuming alcohol during the whole month, we will stay together. But, if you drink, I will leave you. God instructed me in a dream that if you don't quit drinking, I must leave, and I will!"

Furthermore, Trudy decided to get tough and insisted that we partially separate. She would stay in the bedroom downstairs, and I would take the upstairs bedroom. I complied and she reminded me of the ultimatum: if I could not stop drinking, we would separate, and she would move back to Saskatchewan while I stayed in Alberta. I knew she was serious.

It baffles the mind as to what addicted people will do to satisfy their addiction. As an alcoholic, the temptation was so severe that it drove me to the point where I had to decide if I was willing to risk it all to feed my addiction. To my great shame, that is exactly what I did.

As I look back, I wonder if, at that time, I subconsciously wanted Trudy to catch me drinking. I kept a bottle of alcohol hidden behind my night table next to my bed, and then left it there when I went on a trip, even though I knew she would search my room while I was gone. Besides continuing to drink at home, my alcohol consumption intensified while on long layovers. I was nearing destruction and felt like there was nothing I could do about it. So, the inevitable happened. After I returned from a trip, Trudy confronted me. She said that she had found the alcohol in my room, and she knew I was still carousing and drinking while at work. She told me we had to call the children and inform them that we were separating. I agreed without even attempting to defend myself. After all, I knew she was right.

We made the terribly difficult but necessary call to the family and told them of our plans to separate. Our daughter Priscilla told her mother that they had suspected that a separation was inevitable and insisted that her mom come and live with them. The first portion of her dream was being fulfilled: the rest would also be fulfilled exactly as laid out in the dream.

Our separation, though amicable, was extremely difficult for both of us. On the one hand, I was crushed to realize that my

BOB MCLAUGHLIN

marriage was on the rocks and possibly would be totally over. Yet on the other hand, now that I was separated, I could drink as much as I wanted to without giving account to anyone. I wasted no time in satisfying my selfish desires. I became everything that, as a child, I had sworn I would never become. And now, here I was. I had become just like my father – living a life of total debauchery.

Trudy told me she cried during the entire trip all the way from Alberta to our daughter's home in Saskatchewan. However, everything God laid out in the dream came true. God's hand and provision were with Trudy.

Chapter 31

BOB, GOD IS NOT FINISHED WITH YOU YET

Several years had passed since I last met with my friend and mentor, Leander. I first met him in 1983 when I was a Bible college student on the prairies of Saskatchewan, Canada. Each morning before classes began, the entire student body would gather for morning chapel. The speaker that autumn morning was Leander. He was introduced as the national director of a prominent mission organization with Canadian headquarters located in Eastern Canada. I was immediately impressed with his message and manner.

Following the chapel service that morning, I introduced myself and asked if we could have a coffee together sometime before he left campus. We arranged to meet later that afternoon at the roadside restaurant and service station down by the highway. At the time I had no idea he would become a dear and trusted friend, nor did I know that he would eventually become significantly involved in our future evangelistic ministry.

In 1986, a year before I graduated from Bible college, Trudy and I incorporated a non-profit evangelistic organization and Leander became chairman of the board of directors, a position he held for sixteen years.

BOB MCLAUGHLIN

Now, many years later, we were about to meet again. Frankly, I had no desire to meet with him or anyone connected with the church or Christianity in general. By this time, due to my sin, I had lost the successful international ministry which God had given to me. The respect of the Christian community that I once craved, and had, was also gone. I had become everything I swore I would never become. I had broken every vow I had made to God, the church, my board of directors and Trudy. And now, Trudy and I were separated, and I was at an all time low. In this dark and depressing time in my life, alcohol seemed like my only real friend, but it was taking its toll on me.

For some time, Leander wondered where I was and how I was doing. His persistence eventually paid off and he was able to track me down in Alberta. At the time, I was working as a flight attendant with a Canadian airline. When Trudy and I separated, I had moved into a house with several pilots who worked for the same airline. All of us were going through a variety of difficult issues in our personal lives and some, like me, had a serious drinking problem.

The house was nothing short of a total party house. On our days off, most of us were drunk. To my great shame, I had willingly become an active participant in this den of iniquity. The vices I had quit years before, when I became a born-again Christian, had now returned with a vengeance and they were destroying my life.

During my first few weeks in the house, we all partied strong and hard. Lots of alcohol and music filled the house and our parties became very popular with other employees. Sometimes the partying would last all night with the occasional visit from the police for noise disturbance. This lifestyle eventually began wearing on each of us and personalities began clashing.

Not surprisingly, it eventually became clear to everyone that I was undoubtedly the number one alcoholic in the house. Though I was the first to be tagged with that title, it was my opinion that most of the residents in that house had serious issues with alcohol.

218

IN THE WAR

And because of my reputation, whenever there was a mess following a party, I was inevitably the one accused of being the most responsible.

It was during this time that I received the phone call from Leander. He informed me he was in town on business and invited me to join him for a meeting at a local restaurant. I told him I was in no condition to meet with him. He told me it mattered not what condition I was in, he still wanted to meet with me. I tried without success to convince him that I was unworthy of a visit with him. His loving persistence paid off once again and I agreed to meet him for breakfast the next morning.

Well, the next morning I woke up extremely hungover. Surprisingly, I did remember that I was to meet Leander. I immediately consumed a fair amount of alcohol, seeking its liquid courage for my scheduled breakfast appointment and to help calm my alcoholic morning shakes. Consumption of alcohol in the morning on my days off had become a common practice for the past few months. That morning as I drank, I was keenly aware of my addiction to alcohol. But frankly, I just did not care anymore. I was quickly on my way to hitting absolute bottom, as described in any 12-step program for addicts. I knew all this because I had been through rehab not long before. Six months after graduating from rehab I was drunk again.

I arrived at Leander's hotel, and he embraced me saying how glad he was to see me. I knew that I stunk from the stench of alcohol, along with the smell of stale tobacco, but he did not mention it nor allow it to faze him. We walked the short distance to a nearby restaurant and sat down at a table. I'm sure our server was not amused with the smells emanating from our table as she took our order. I am equally sure she found it even more frustrating to realize that she would have to clean up our table once we left. After all, I was really making a mess. I was spilling coffee every time that I lifted my cup, with shaking hands, to my lips. Leander was also

219

struggling with spilling coffee; however, his shaking was due to Parkinson's disease, not alcoholism.

Leander sat and listened for the next hour and a half as I wept while telling him how I had turned my back on God and His church, and how terribly far I had fallen into iniquity and sin. I told him Trudy and I were separated, and it did not look like anything could be fixed. I was so ashamed of myself that I did not feel worthy to even be in his presence. I told him there was no longer any hope for me, but he never condemned nor rebuked me. He just listened.

When we finished breakfast, we walked outside to the parking lot. I lit a cigarette and suddenly Leander wrapped his arms tightly around me and said, "Bob, God is not finished with you yet!" I began to weep as these words penetrated my soul. "Leander," I responded, "I'm done! There is no hope for me anymore. Please forgive me and thank you for never giving up on me."

Before we went our separate ways that morning, he repeated those words to me, "Bob, God is not finished with you yet!"

The party house eventually became too much for me. I needed to get out of there and find a place of my own. I reasoned that, if I was on my own, no one would complain about my drinking and then there would be no more tension – I could do as I wished. So, I found a small, one-room apartment in a small town a few miles outside of the city. Once I got settled in my new place, I began thinking that, even though I could now drink all I wanted without people complaining, maybe, just maybe I could cut back a bit or even quit altogether. After all, I had successfully done it before.

In the airline industry flight attendants can trade shifts with other employees. As a classic alcoholic I decided to go on one more major drinking spree before attempting to change my life. To accomplish this, I traded a full month's worth of shifts, which allowed me nearly an entire month off to accommodate my plan to drink to my heart's content. But that month almost did me in. Every day I walked to one of the three liquor stores in the small

IN THE WAR

town and purchased two or three bottles of wine. Once I was back in my apartment I began to drink, often to the point of passing out. It eventually got so bad that I would lose track of time and would make numerous telephone calls, racking up my cell phone bill.

I have some vivid and some hazy memories of demonic visitations where I would engage in conversations with them. I knew they were out to kill me. The Bible speaks of demons and the devil two hundred and twenty-seven times. They are real and are God's enemies as well as ours. Jesus said, *"The thief comes only to steal and kill and destroy; I came that they may have life and have it abundantly."* (John 10:10 NASB) This thief was stealing, killing, and destroying me and these demonic encounters frightened me, so then I would drink even more. Yet, during those days I would often cry and confess to Jesus that I was sorry for turning away from Him. I would tell Him to please just take me out of this life of misery. This went on day after day for twenty-three days.

It was February 26, 2005, when I woke up, hungover once again. Frankly, I was amazed I was still alive. For a few minutes I just lay there and stared at the ceiling. I remember thinking how surprised I was that I felt as good as I did. I reached beside my bed for a bottle, hoping there was a little alcohol left in it. I swung my legs over the side of the bed, sat up and drank the last few swallows of wine that were left in that bottle. After a couple of minutes, I stood to walk to the bathroom. I managed to take perhaps five steps when my legs went out from under me. I collapsed to the floor and began shaking violently. I vomited blood and messed myself front and behind. I was a basket case and fear filled my heart.

There is no doubt in my mind that at that point God intervened on my behalf, and a few minutes later, He gave me the strength to call Alcoholics Anonymous. An hour or two later I was having coffee with an AA member. Yes, February 26, 2005, was the last day I consumed alcohol.

Over the next two years, that beautiful and almost unbelievable phrase, "Bob, God is not finished with you yet!" would come to me supernaturally and unsolicited, through four individuals independently of each other. Here is how I remember them.

It was still dark outside when my alarm went off at 4:00 AM. I was glad to have had two full days to recuperate and get over my shakes. I always tried to have at least one full day of sobriety before reporting for my duties as a flight attendant.

Once again, I put on my flight uniform, drove to the airport, and reported for duty. As I recall, our four-day pairing began with a morning flight to Vancouver, BC. I checked in at our airline's crew room to meet with the crew for our pre-flight meeting. Following the meeting, we made our way to the plane and did our pre-flight checks, making sure everything was flightworthy before boarding our passengers and departing for Vancouver.

On this first day of four days of flying, I was the lead flight attendant. Once we were ready, we began the boarding procedure. As lead flight attendant, I stood at the front to greet each guest with a smile as I checked their boarding pass. When everyone was on board, we received permission from the captain to close the main cabin door and begin our safety demonstration, while the ground crew proceeded with our push back from the gate.

Once we were in Vancouver and all the passengers were deplaned, we had a small break before our next flight, which would take us to Regina, Saskatchewan. I took my break in the airport smoking room. After freshening up, I made my way back to our aircraft and once again we began the boarding process.

One by one I greeted each passenger and checked their boarding pass. After greeting several passengers, I stopped short when I saw the smiling face of my next guest. She handed me her boarding pass as she reached out to give me a big hug. She then looked me in the eyes and said, "Bob, I am so happy to see you. I've been praying for you."

IN THE WAR

With a twinge of shame, I said, "Jean, it's so good to see you too." I continued, "Once we get airborne and I've finished serving my section, I'll come talk to you."

She smiled and said, "Oh good," and then took her seat.

Our flight to Regina was smooth and I finished serving my section of the aircraft. As promised, but with some anxiety and shame, I made my way to where Jean was seated to have a brief talk with her. Jean was a Bible college professor whom I greatly admired.

I knelt beside her aisle seat as she smiled and said, "How are you doing, Bob?"

I knew she was more than aware of my terrible fall into sin and alcoholism, and my separation from Trudy. I realized that she could see the pack of cigarettes in my shirt pocket, but thankfully, she just smiled. Tears began welling up in my eyes as I said, "Jean, my life is terrible. I am living in sin. I drink, I smoke, and I am ashamed of myself. I have brought shame and disgrace to my Lord God, and to my wife, my family, and the church." I looked at her as I continued, "I am so sorry, Jean. I hope you can find it in your heart to forgive me."

As I began to get up, Jean reached out with her hand, and gently grabbed my shoulder, and said, "Bob, God is not finished with you yet!"

As I choked back the tears, I returned to the forward galley and prepared for our landing. Frankly, I was shocked and could hardly believe that she had said those words to me. They were the same words that Leander had shared with me, just days before. Our flight landed in Regina and as Jean was getting off the plane, she looked me in the eyes, smiled, and said, "Bob, don't forget what I told you. Remember, God is not finished with you yet!"

That night, in my hotel room, I wept. I fell asleep wondering if God was trying to tell me something. *Was it possible that He really was not finished with me?*

BOB MCLAUGHLIN

Another time, I was given the same message but this time with an amazing addition.

As I recall, we were on the last flight of the day while on another four-day pairing. Earlier in the day, when we first met as a crew, I was pleased to see that I would be working with one crew member whom I had worked with in the past. Her name was Bonnie, and she was a nice Christian woman and pleasant to work with.

This last flight was a redeye from Vancouver, BC to Toronto, Ontario. As flight attendants we recognized the pros and cons of an all-night redeye flight. One pro was that once we finished serving the passengers, most of them usually went to sleep for the night. A con was that there was not a lot to do and consequently it could be an exceptionally long and boring flight.

A day or two earlier, I had handwritten a few paragraphs which I titled "A Spiritual Quest." I had brought it with me as it was a work in progress. An hour or so into our flight that night, and once our service was completed, I approached Bonnie and asked her if she would consider reading my draft and giving me her candid opinion of it. I was pleased when she said, "I would be happy to do that, Bob."

A few minutes later she came to me, smiling as she said that she would like to discuss what I wrote. I answered, "Great!" and poured myself a cup of coffee before we took our seats in the forward galley.

Bonnie looked at me and said, "Bob, I don't tell many people this, but I believe I have a special prophetic gift." She continued, "I read what you wrote, and God spoke to me as I finished reading each page. The word I heard from God was the word 'five!'" Then she said, "I am also to inform you that, Bob, God is not finished with you yet!"

I looked at her and said, "Really?"

She continued, "And the number 'five' is related to the fact that God will raise you up again to preach."

"So, the number five is a time frame, so to speak?" I questioned.

"Yes!" she responded.

224

IN THE WAR

"That means God is going to raise me up again in five something. Will it be five days from now?"

"No!" was her answer.

I continued, "Well then, do you mean five weeks?"

Again, her answer was, "No!"

I asked, "Well, do you mean in five months?"

And again, her answer was a firm, "No!"

I looked at her and exclaimed, "Five years?"

Bonnie smiled and said, "Yes Bob, in five years you will be preaching again. This is the message from God for you." I was excited but disappointed at the time frame. I thanked Bonnie.

A third unsolicited event, when I would hear that phrase yet again, occurred while I was still employed with the airline. Ironically, I was again the lead flight attendant, operating a flight to beautiful Prince Edward Island.

I believe that this time we were at Toronto Pearson International Airport in Ontario. As I began the boarding process, I greeted the guests and checked their boarding passes. To my great surprise, I immediately recognized the gentleman as he handed me his boarding pass. For many years Dr. Ralph Bell had been an associate evangelist of the BGEA but was now retired. He saw the look of surprise on my face and then his eyes widened as he said, "Bob, what on earth are you doing here?" Before I could answer, he gave me a big hug.

My eyes began to tear up as I asked, "Ralph, may I come talk with you shortly after we get airborne?"

With a concerned look on his face, he replied, "Bob, I would love to talk with you."

After our flight took off, I asked one of my colleagues if they would consider servicing my section during the flight so that I could talk with Ralph. I was pleased when he responded, "Yes, of course, Bob." Ralph's wife was more than kind enough to allow me

225

to steal her husband away for the duration of the flight. I poured us a coffee and we sat in an empty back row.

Ralph and I met several years earlier during one of Dr. Graham's evangelistic crusades. At that time, Ralph asked me if I would like to join him at the nearby prison where he would be ministering to some prisoners. I was honored and accepted his gracious invitation.

I remember that special meeting very well. The warden only allowed three prisoners to meet with us. Ralph shared his testimony and then he preached a simple message about the story of Zacchaeus. When he finished the message, all three men prayed to receive Christ. On our drive back to the hotel together we rejoiced over the salvation of those three men.

Later that evening, we sat together on Dr. Graham's platform looking out at the thousands of people who came to hear him preach. What impressed me hugely about Dr. Ralph Bell was that while he was preaching to only three men earlier in the day at the prison, he knew that in several hours Billy would be preaching to thousands. I knew there was not a single ounce of jealousy in that humble man of God.

I sat at the back of the aircraft and openly shared everything with Dr. Bell. I told him of my alcoholism, the loss of the ministry and the fact that Trudy and I were currently separated. I told him that I had broken every vow I had ever made to God, the church, my wife, and my family. We both wept as I unfolded my sinful and shameful story.

As I was finishing my story, we had already begun our descent into Charlottetown, PEI. Before I returned to my duties in preparation for landing, I thanked Ralph for allowing me to explain why he saw me in a flight attendant's uniform today. As we stood, Dr. Bell wrapped his arms around me and said, "Bob, God is not finished with you yet!" Stunned at his choice of words, I thanked him again and escorted him back to his seat beside his wife. I apologized to

IN THE WAR

her and thanked her for sharing her husband with me for the flight. With a beautiful smile she said she was happy to have done so.

As our aircraft came to a stop, I finished my arrival announcements. The captain then turned off the seat belt signs, and I opened the main cabin door. Once the stairs were in place and secure, we began to deplane the guests. One by one I said goodbye to each guest as they deplaned. Dr. Bell gave me another hug and said, "Bob, don't forget what I told you." Once on the tarmac he turned, gave me a big smile and a wave before entering the terminal.

Later that night in the hotel, I once again wondered if God was communicating with me through these people. *Is it possible that God is not finished with me yet?* I dared not hope.

The next time I heard those words was even more of a surprise to me. Here is how I remember it unfolding.

I was back in Saskatchewan for a few days so my wife and I could attend one of our marriage counselling sessions, when I received a telephone call from a total stranger. He was an eighteen-year-old young man who was visiting his mom in a small Saskatchewan city. He told me he had been informed that I was driving to Alberta in a couple days. I replied that yes, I would be driving to Alberta and asked how I could help him. He said, "I am a Bible college student, and I need a ride to the college which is just on the outskirts of western Calgary. May I catch a ride with you, Mr. McLaughlin?"

I responded that he most likely would not enjoy a ride with me as I was a smoker and I planned on smoking the entire trip back to Alberta. He said, "I do not mind if you smoke. I promise you it will not bother me. May I catch a ride with you please?"

I replied, "OK, but you must understand that the most I will do is crack the window a bit for you."

I arranged to pick him up and together we began our seven-hour drive. An hour or so into the drive, as I smoked one cigarette after another, he said, "Mr. McLaughlin, would you consider sharing your story with me?" I looked at him, squinted with my

227

eyes and responded, "Young man, you really don't want to hear my wretched story!"

He was silent for a few minutes and then said, "Mr. McLaughlin, I do want to hear your story – really I do."

I studied his face and replied, "Okay, hang on tight young man! You asked for it!" and I commenced to totally unload my entire shameful story on him. I was sure he fully understood that I was still harboring some anger toward the body of Christ, the Church. I was impressed that he did not interrupt me, not even one time, as I rambled on during the whole trip.

When we arrived at the Bible college, he opened the car door and thanked me for the ride and for sharing my whole story with him. After he got out, he started to close the door but stopped and opened it wide. He leaned in and said, "Mr. McLaughlin, may I tell you what God told me during our ride here today?" I looked at him scoffingly and thought to myself, *what could this eighteen-year-old possibly tell me?* I continued to look at him in silence as he went on, "I have a message for you from God."

I almost said, "Sure, humor me," but instead, I replied, "Sure, tell me what you think God wants you to say to me." He smiled and continued, "Mr. McLaughlin, God told me to tell you that He is going to raise you up again. God also said to be sure to tell you that, 'God is not finished with you yet!'"

In almost total disbelief, I looked at his smiling face as he thanked me again for the ride and then shut the door. I watched him walk away and disappear into one of the buildings. As I slowly drove out of the parking lot the question in my mind was, *just who was that young man?* I do wonder today if perhaps he was yet another angel, divinely appointed to ride with me in a smoke-filled car for seven hours and listen to my story but also, more importantly, to deliver a message to me from God.

It is utterly amazing how God orchestrates His will in our lives to accomplish His greater good as well as *our* greater good. God's

Word says, *"And we know that God causes all things to work together for good to those who love God, to those who are called according to His purpose."* (Romans 8:28 NASB) The Bible also says in Isaiah 46:11b, *"Truly I have spoken; truly I will bring it to pass. I have planned it, surely I will do it."* (NASB) I can now testify that it was none other than God who delivered those unsolicited messages to me through His chosen servants. I can also testify that He *was not* finished with me and five years after my conversation with Bonnie, I was preaching the gospel once again.

Bob and Trudy with Leander

Chapter 32

A 12-STEP PROGRAM BEGS THE QUESTION TO THE CHURCH: FORGIVENESS – SEVENTY TIMES SEVEN – WHERE ART THOU?

It was the afternoon of February 26, 2005. After being on a month-long drinking spree I was weak and vomiting blood. Though extremely sick, I managed to walk to a nearby restaurant where I was going to meet with an AA member who I had connected with by telephone earlier that day.

As we sat in that roadside restaurant, he could not help but notice just how sick I really was. He became rather adamant that he should take me to the hospital to dry out. I, on the other hand, was just as adamant that I did not want to go to the hospital. I told him that I'd rather he helped me by taking me to an AA meeting. He readily agreed and an hour later, he took me to a meeting nearby.

Together we drove to the meeting while I remained extremely sick and shaky. When we arrived, I was hesitant, at first, to even enter the meeting room. But, with some encouragement from my new friend, I took a seat at the table, and he poured a cup of coffee for me. As I sat there and timidly looked around the room, I cradled the cup of coffee in my shaking hands while I slowly and carefully sipped on it.

I scanned the faces around the table and noticed an older gentleman sitting across from me, smiling from ear to ear. "Hello, Bob!" he said, in a gruff and raspy voice, as if he knew me. When I heard his voice, I vaguely remembered hearing it before but could not figure out why or how or when. I also wondered how he knew my name. Eventually I learned that he was one of the AA fellows I had contacted and apparently, I had called him several times over the last week. In fact, some of those calls were extremely late at night and woke him up, causing him to bark at me to "dump out the booze and go to sleep!"

The AA meeting commenced, as usual, with the chairman reading the 12 Steps followed by the reminder that anything which is seen or heard in that room is to remain in the room. It was important that we not discuss anything outside of the AA meeting regarding anything we heard someone say or anyone we saw in the meeting. Everyone was to remain anonymous, respecting each person who openly shared his cares and concerns. After giving these instructions the chairman asked the person next to him to begin the sharing time. We were then to continue going around the room, one by one, sharing anything we desired to share. We also had the option to remain silent and listen if we so desired.

When it came to me, I began with, "My name is Bob, and I am an alcoholic." I was a complete wreck, and my body was trembling, but I continued to speak. I babbled on and on, sharing my whole story, and of course, blaming everyone and everything for all my problems, including my marriage, which was clearly on the rocks. Eventually I was done whining about everything, and I shut up. Everyone kindly listened, having heard so many newcomers share the same old story which, ironically, would inevitably neglect the obvious problem of alcohol consumption. It was classic alcoholic babble.

IN THE WAR

Following the AA meeting I went for a visit with the man who had brought me to the meeting. To my surprise, the older gentleman with the gruff and raspy voice came along as well. It turned out that he was a rather highly respected member of AA and had twenty years of sobriety and experience with the program. Over those years he had sponsored a good number of desperate men with addictions.

As we were talking, I didn't know that this man was about to have a profound influence on my life, but then he offered to be my sponsor. He let me know that he had some firm guidelines I had to follow if I desired his sponsorship and if he caught me in a lie, then he would no longer sponsor me. At the time, I thought this was rather harsh but decided I would ask him to sponsor me. Little did I realize how, over the next two and a half years, he would help me work through the 12-step program, living one day at a time. This man utterly understood me and consequently knew exactly how to help me. Though he was tough on me, it was obvious that he cared. He told me to contact him, no matter the time of day or night, if I was even the slightest bit tempted to consume alcohol.

Those first few weeks were extremely difficult for me. I remember getting squirrely one night, all alone in my one-room apartment. I was weakening and realized I needed to call my sponsor, despite the time of night. With my hand shaking, I dialed his number and told him I was struggling. He responded with, "Get down to the sidewalk! I will pick you up in five minutes!" I put my coat on, went to wait for him, and sure enough he came, and drove us to an all-night coffee shop. For more than two hours we sat there drinking coffee and talking. He listened intently and responded appropriately to my every comment. He shared about his personal struggle with alcohol, and I was fascinated with his brutal honesty.

This man became a true friend and confidant, and over the next two and a half years, I spent many hours with him. On my days off, when I was not flying, I could be found spending time with my sponsor. I was amazed and thankful for his obvious commitment to help me. It meant that even if I needed to contact him from a distant city, he would be available 24/7. Now that was true commitment – something the church, in general, could learn from.

As I thought about the kind of commitment that long-term members of the AA program clearly possess, I could not help but think about the church. Jesus made it very clear that the body of Christ, i.e., the church, was to be the epitome of forgiveness. We read about this in the book of Matthew, chapter 18. Here Jesus responds to a question posed by none other than Peter. *"Then Peter came and said to Him, 'Lord, how often shall my brother sin against me and I forgive him? Up to seven times?' Jesus said to him, 'I do not say to you, up to seven times, but up to seventy times seven.'"* (Matthew 18:21-22 NASB) Wow, what a statement!

What I know from my many years of involvement with the 12-step program is that the door to these AA meeting rooms is always open. In other words, everyone, no matter how many times they fail, is always welcomed back with open arms. I have personally witnessed several individuals who accomplished a year or two of sobriety and then, sadly, fell back into their addiction. They slowly made their way back to the meeting rooms and were always received with joy.

Evangelical churches, on the other hand, often do not do the same. When a member of the church falls into sin, many times they are shunned and, in essence, they feel excommunicated. That is virtually like being thrown into a stormy sea without a life preserver. When questioned why they would turn their backs on such people, some have responded that those individuals are simply reaping what they have sown. Forgiveness, as commanded by Jesus, seems to be missing in the church when this happens.

Sadly, many of those who are shunned by churches never make their way back, and those who attempt to return find the doors rather difficult to re-enter. There are some, like me, who have

IN THE WAR

managed to make their way back, but they often find the reception is not sunshine, lollipops, and rainbows, so to speak. This begs a question to the church in general: forgiveness–seventy times seven–where art thou?

Chapter 33

REPENTANCE, COUNSELING, AND A RESTORED MARRIAGE

I remember that after only two weeks of sobriety, I decided to share the good news with my dear wife, Trudy, as well as to inform her of my plans to return home immediately. I was so excited, and I distinctly remember the conversation. I called her number and she answered. With great excitement and a rather presumptuous attitude and tone of voice I said, "Hi hon – well I'm finally sober and attending AA meetings, and I've not had a drink for two weeks. So, I thought you would be pleased to know I am coming home, a sober man." I then paused, and the silence for the next few moments was a bit concerning and frankly, disturbing. *After all,* I thought, *she should be over the moon with excitement and anticipation of the imminent return of her man.* As the irritating silence continued, I thought that perhaps I simply needed to repeat my exciting news. I was about to do just that when the silence was finally broken.

In a sweet but unusually firm voice, Trudy said, "No, you are not coming home! In fact, let me tell you what is going to happen. You will faithfully continue to attend AA meetings for the next two years. You will remain faithful to me and will attend professional, Christian marriage counselling with me over the next two years as well! Then, after a full two years, and only after two years, I will decide, and let you know, if you can or cannot come home. Do you understand?"

As her searing words burned into my brain, rage and fury brought my Gaelic, Irish blood to a boil. I immediately threw my cell phone across the room, smashing it against the wall. I shouted out loud, "What's wrong with her? How dare she throw ice water on my great accomplishments; I cannot believe the audacity of that woman! Man, she makes me so angry!" Clearly, at that point, I was fit to be tied.

I got into my car and drove over to my sponsor's house. Once I was inside, and to my great shame, I began whining and shouting with my arms flailing as I unfolded the entire story to my sponsor in extremely colorful and explicit words.

My sponsor just sat there and listened with a grin on his face. Eventually he asked, "Are you finished?"

I continued for a little longer but eventually I slumped down in a chair and sat there, shaking. As I looked at him, I got even angrier because of his smile. It seemed like the more I got angry, the broader his smile became. Suddenly, to my utter astonishment, he burst out in very disturbing and loud laughter. I was dumbfounded at his response. In all honesty, I wanted to punch him square in the nose – but I refrained.

Once my sponsor stopped laughing, he deliberately locked eyes with me and shouted, "Just what did you expect her to do? Can't you, for a moment, understand the pain and agony you put that poor woman through? Tell me one good reason why she should even consider allowing you back into her life." He continued, "What's really amazing is how she managed to put up with you and your drinking and shameful carousing for all those painful years." As those hurtful but accurate words sank into my brain, I began to weep, a broken man with my foolish pride exposed and crushed. He continued, "Bob, we have a lot of work to do and maybe, just maybe,

IN THE WAR

if you agree to go along with her requests and you work hard at the 12-step program, she may take you back – but don't count on it." He continued, "Bob, you need to earn back her respect!"

I knew he was right, so with a subdued voice I responded, "Okay. Let's do this!"

Following that pivotal visit with my new sponsor, I drove back to my one-room apartment. I walked up the flight of stairs, opened my door, and promptly fell prostrate on the floor, weeping and crying out to the Lord. Through genuine tears of repentance, I confessed all my sin, and sought God's mercy, forgiveness, and cleansing. As I lay on the floor, tears of joy streamed from my eyes, and for the next few minutes, God's holy presence filled the room. His forgiveness washed over me with unprecedented waves, filling me with a peace that only comes from the Lord Jesus. For the first time in a long time, I felt the fullness of God's Holy Spirit. Eventually I sat up, opened my Bible, and turned to 1 John 1:9 where it says, *"If we confess our sins, He is faithful and righteous, to forgive us our sins and to cleanse us from all unrighteousness."* (NASB) By faith, I took God at His Word and stood to my feet, a forgiven and cleansed man.

I called Trudy and apologized for everything I had done. I told her that I had truly repented and if her offer still stood, I was willing to follow her explicit instructions for the entire two years. Thankfully, she agreed.

We contacted a Christian marriage counselor and began meeting with him right away. Our counselor developed a plan for each of us and for the first few weeks we met with him separately. Later, when he thought we were ready, he arranged for us together to meet with him. Frankly, at first, I found it rather difficult to trust him, not because of him personally, but simply because of past situations involving broken trust. However, over time he won my trust, and I allowed his wise counsel to help me both personally and in our marriage.

239

BOB McLAUGHLIN

The two years passed quickly, even though at times it seemed like they would take forever. The days, weeks, and months were filled with my job as a flight attendant, AA meetings, and appointments with my sponsor when I was home in Alberta.

About a year and a half into the two-year timeframe, an incident, which would change things, took place while I was working on one of my flights – I had an attack of vertigo. I called the captain and he had me come to the flight deck where he administered oxygen to me and then decided it would be best if I was off-loaded in Calgary. Once I arrived home, I contacted the company doctor and arranged an appointment. It was determined that I needed some time off. The vertigo was so bad at times that I would fall to the ground from dizziness, or I would lie on my bed or the floor with the whole world continuously spinning.

After two weeks the company doctor decided that I was fit to return to work. I protested, stating that my condition if anything, had worsened rather than improved. I talked with my company team leader, and he suggested that I seek medical advice from my personal doctor. As a result of the worsening vertigo, I attempted to get a different position with the company. However, over time they recommended that I resign and seek employment elsewhere. I complied and therefore was unemployed for a few weeks.

Since we were close to the two-year mark given by Trudy and because I had honored her instructions, she invited me to return home. So, at long last we were reunited as husband and wife. Her tough love strategy worked, and we were once again a loving and happy couple. All glory, honor, and praise to God! It is clear to us that it was only through the miraculous work of our Holy God that a couple, who was separated for three and a half years, could get back together. Indeed, God was not finished using us.

I wrote about how I had repented and was blessed with cleansing, forgiveness, and the fullness of the Holy Spirit. However, when a minister of the gospel falls into deep sin, as in my case,

IN THE WAR

there is, in my opinion, a definite need for public repentance. To be honest, at the time I really was not seeking an opportunity to repent publicly – but our God arranged one.

In those days Trudy and I were attending a large church in a nearby city. Over our years of ministering, I had preached in nearly every evangelical church in that city. The church we were currently attending was no exception and nearly everyone who went to that church knew who I was and had heard me preach a fair number of times.

It was a typical Sunday morning as we drove to church. Frankly, we were not expecting the amazing blessing we were about to receive. We entered the church and, as was our habit, we walked up the stairs to the balcony and selected our seats in the last row at the very top. The service began as usual, so we settled in and anticipated a well-preached message from the senior pastor of the church, and we were not disappointed. His message was so clear. It was a simple three-point sermon but was so anointed by an unusual presence of the Holy Spirit. When he finished, he extended a public invitation for anyone who sensed God's Holy Spirit prompting and piercing their heart to repent, to stand and make their way to the front of the church.

At that point, an unusual prompting from God came over me and it was as if He lifted me out of my seat and to my feet. I felt as if it was not my human strength that was enabling me to stand, but that it was clearly God Himself. Once I was standing, I said to Trudy, "I have to go down to the front."

It was a surreal moment, and the following is exactly how it all unfolded. I walked down the steps of the balcony and through a door to two flights of stairs which took me down to the first floor. Another door opened to the foyer where I entered one of two doorways into the sanctuary and faced an aisle that led up to the platform. As I nearly floated down that long aisle, I vaguely remember hearing several people whispering. When I arrived at the front of

BOB MCLAUGHLIN

the church, I fell to my knees on the platform stairs and wept – publicly repenting of my sin.

I noticed that my dear wife had joined me, as well as a few people who laid hands on us and prayed for us. We stood and rejoiced over all that God had just done and we were overjoyed as we reflected on all that had happened over the last couple of years: 1) I had repented privately, and God forgave me and filled me with His Spirit. 2) Not only had God restored me, but He also restored our marriage. 3) Now I had repented publicly in a church where nearly all the people present knew me and the sin into which I had fallen.

Yet after all this, God was about to do something more – something I thought He would never do. He was going to allow me to go back into ministry.

PART SEVEN

ADVERSITY CONTINUES AS HUNDREDS OF THOUSANDS ARE COMING TO CHRIST

Chapter 34

A Slow Cautious Return

The joy of our marriage had returned and by God's grace and mercy (and in part because of my personal and public repentance) my relationship with my Lord was truly glorious and renewed. Life was good once again. Yet I was still unemployed. At this point I was in my mid-fifties, and frankly it was not easy starting over again. We prayed daily that the Lord would provide suitable employment. I turned in my Bible to one of my favorite passages of scripture and read Proverbs 3:5-6. *"Trust in the LORD with all your heart and do not lean on your own understanding. In all your ways acknowledge Him, and He will make your paths straight."* (NASB). We were determined to acknowledge Him, and we were going to trust Him to guide and direct us to His chosen employment for me.

Though I had applied for employment with several companies it was to no avail. So, we continued praying and searching. Just as I was beginning to wonder if I would find a job, my son-in-law told me that he had noticed a job offer online with the Salvation Army. I thought, is it possible that my God was going to allow me back into ministry? We prayed about it, and I completed the application and applied.

BOB MCLAUGHLIN

After only a couple of days I received a telephone call from the Major of the Salvation Army. He said "Bob, we have reviewed your application and have contacted your references, and therefore we have decided to invite you to take the position." I immediately accepted, and a few days later I began my new position in the Family Service department as Trustee for many needy individuals. These individuals were appointed to the Family Service department by Social Services. Over the first few days I was introduced to each of my clients and their social workers and developed a good working relationship with them and their department.

For the next two and a half years I was honored and privileged to provide this unique and special service for these dear needy individuals. It was clearly not an easy job but nonetheless it was a unique ministry and I wholeheartedly jumped into it.

Many of my clients possessed a variety of mental health challenges as well as life threatening addictions. However, there were others who simply found themselves in a difficult time in their lives and simply needed help in budgeting and managing their resources. Some of these were successful in following and complying with our guidelines and over time were able to cut their ties with us.

Aside from my usual duties of meeting most clients once a week, it was our goal to help them over time to wean off government assistance and become independent people contributing to society rather than being forever dependent on government assistance. Of course, it was understood that some clientele would always need this benevolent government assistance. For the most part, my relationship with each client was good. Over time I developed a deep love for each of them.

Unfortunately, there were also those who had developed cunning and deceitful habits after being in the system for a good number of years. In essence, they had perfected the art of deception and were able to con Social Services and thus abuse the system. I had been warned of these individuals by my predecessor and the

246

IN THE WAR

assigned social workers during my introduction to this unique ministry. Yet my own personal issues as a recovering alcoholic were clearly an asset in this ministry. It helped immensely to detect their deception. But of course, I was not always successful.

It was not long before they attempted to push the envelope as far as possible in their almost daily desire to beat the system. Sadly, it was my opinion that the system in many cases failed these individuals.

After a couple years with the Salvation Army, I received a surprise and unsolicited call from an old friend in Alaska. He and I had first met back in our Bible college days. His call came with a challenge. As Area Director of a Northern ministry, he asked me to pray about joining him for a unique and extremely difficult ministry.

We prayed about this new and intriguing challenge and sensed the Lord's leading in it. Shortly thereafter my friend arranged for me to fly to Alaska for a vision trip to see firsthand this unique northern ministry and to clarify the scope of the challenge.

The challenge was huge. My friend was seeking someone to mobilize Christians to be fulltime missionaries devoting themselves to live in a difficult region of the globe, a vast area of the world stretching from the west coast of Alaska across northern Canada to Greenland. This vast area is sparsely populated and, in many parts, spiritually dark.

This challenge possessed three exceedingly difficult components. One was the fact that this area is part of America and Canada, and because these two countries are considered Christian, they were not considered an area needing to be reached with the gospel. Of course, this is clearly a wrong perception, yet that is for the most part how the church views America and Canada. The second challenge is the fact that this area of the world for the most part does not appeal to people as a place they would desire to live as career missionaries. The third challenge is to make sure the

247

potential missionaries know they are called by God to the unique and difficult challenges in serving Him in a most unforgiven region of the world.

Upon my return from the vision trip to Alaska, Trudy and I sought the Lord's will daily in prayer as well as counsel from Christian leaders. Over time we believed God would have us move in this new direction.

My friend felt it best if we joined the Canadian branch of their mission which would allow us to continue living in Canada and enable us to better recruit resources for the northern ministry. This would propose a unique marriage between the Canadian mission and the far north mission. Though both ministries belonged to the same international mission, they were clearly different. Thus, there was a potential for territorial issues to arise.

After discussing this potential ministry with the Canadian Director, they agreed to its possibility. Realising the potential detriment of territorial issues arising, our friend arranged for a face-to-face sit-down meeting to discuss this possible joint effort before pursuing it further.

The meeting was a rather intense 5 hours. However, it ended well with a firm understanding that we were to be loyal to the mission as a mobilizer and staff member. Our position would be focused on mobilizing resources specifically for the northern mission. I knew at that point that there could be some future issues in attempting to merge the two missions, but we all agreed it could be done.

We made application with the Mission and once accepted we resigned from the Salvation Army and began trusting God for the prayer and financial support needed to conduct this new mission. We were thrilled to be back in full time ministry again.

Over the next few months, the Lord provided the support needed and we sold our home in Saskatchewan and moved to Manitoba to begin our new mission.

IN THE WAR

Unfortunately, it was not long before we began seeing the foundation of the agreement between the north and the south ministries begin to deteriorate.

Everything was new to us. A new ministry, a new town, a new home, finding a new church. We were beginning a new chapter in our lives, and we were excited.

We had recently moved to a little farming community southeast of Winnipeg, Manitoba.

Shortly after we settled into our new home, we were invited to travel to the Canadian arctic to explore opportunities related to our new ministry.

The Arctic community of Kugluktuk is located approximately 1,000 kilometers due north of Edmonton, Alberta, Canada, and situated on the shores of the Coronation gulf of the Arctic Ocean.

This Arctic community with a population of 1,500 people, of which approximately ninety percent are Inuit/Eskimo. I was oblivious to what God was going to do over the next few years.

Upon landing at the tiny airport, we were driven to our accommodations. The entire community was interconnected with gravel roads which were wet and muddy. Though it was cold, being early October, things were not fully frozen yet. Once we settled in, we were served a wonderful meal in the restaurant and retired for the night.

Early the next morning after breakfast I approached my friend who was getting ready to leave for the worksite and asked if he wanted me to go with him. I was a bit taken aback when he replied, "I don't have time for you. You just need to get out and about and make yourself known in this community. I'll see you tonight." And out the door he went with his work crew. I love a challenge, so undaunted I went to my room and put on my coat and out the door I went not having the slightest idea where to go or who to see. After walking the muddy streets for a few minutes, I asked a young Inuit lady in passing if she knew how I could find the Minister of the

249

Anglican church. At the time this was the only functioning church in the hamlet. To my surprise, she not only knew who the minister was, but wrote out his name and telephone number for me. I hurried back to the inn and called the number. It turned out that this fellow was not really the minister but was a lay reader in the Anglican church and was the acting minister as the church was without one. He agreed to show me around the community and told me he would pick me up in a few minutes and to wait just outside the inn. He pulled up on his 4-wheeler quad. After a warm greeting I hopped on the back and off we went.

He drove me all around the community pointing out all the sites. After an hour or so we came back to the inn. For the next 3 hours, we sat drinking coffee while he told me a little about himself and the community in general. He informed me that the church had been without a minister for a couple years and that he was doing the best he could as the acting lay reader. He seemed excited to know that we were planning on returning to possibly work alongside the church.

The next day the pilot and I walked all around the community and climbed up the huge cliff overlooking the airport and the gulf. As I looked out over this artic community, I wondered if God had great plans for us here in the future.

As this trip came to an end, I sensed the LORD was preparing the way and we were going to have a unique ministry to this community and beyond soon. Upon our return from this rather unexpected and exotic trip to the Arctic, we immediately set our sights on the huge task before us.

Our target was Bible colleges, mission conferences and churches. Because we were new to the area, our friend informed us he would like to help by introducing us to the president of a Bible college located just a few miles from our home.

The meeting was arranged, and our friend picked us up and drove us to the college. We had no idea what was about to happen

IN THE WAR

in this meeting. Trudy and I simply assumed we would be introduced to the president and that itself would open opportunities to have us exposed to the student body as mobilizers.

Once we arrived, the receptionist escorted us to the president's office and our friend introduced us to one another, and we sat down for the meeting. What happened next totally surprised us. After a brief conversation it turned out that we were welcome to recruit students to accompany us to the Arctic for a brief mission.

We were both happy and astonished at how this had all come about. We wasted no time in pursuing this exciting new ministry opportunity. We have always believed the best way to get people excited about ministry is to take them to the field and expose them to the reality of missions. Let them see, smell, and feel it firsthand.

Upon sharing this new opportunity with our Canadian leadership, we discovered there was not the excitement we hoped for. He had inadvertently let on earlier that there were obvious territorial issues between him and the northern ministry especially because the northern ministry's vision cut right through four northern Provinces of Canada, namely the Yukon, Northwest Territories Nunavut, and Nunavik.

Despite some obvious signs of opposition from the Canadian office, we pursued recruiting students from this Bible college to go with us to the Arctic. The students and faculty who went with us over the next few years witnessed an amazing response to the Gospel.

Prior to each mission trip to the Arctic with students, Trudy and I would travel there to do the advance setup work in preparation to ensure the students would experience a successful ministry adventure.

During one of these setup trips, Trudy and I attended the opening of an annual festival event called "Nattiq Frolic's." This weeklong festival is a traditional Inuit welcoming of spring following a long

BOB MCLAUGHLIN

cold and dark winter. It is comprised of traditional games and other Inuit cultural activities.

The opening of the event took place in the Complex Center. We were promptly introduced to the mayor. Upon hearing why, we had come to this Hamlet, he asked if we would be willing to be involved in the opening ceremony that evening. I told him we would be honored. He then brought us up front and introduced us to the audience. To our surprise he invited us to officially open the weeklong festival by cutting the ribbon and to offer an opening prayer to seek God's blessing on the weeklong activities.

Once the evening ended, we were approached by the mayor. He asked us if he could have a word with us. We gladly met with him. To our great surprise he said the following. "Please, my people need to hear about your God. I invite you to come back to my Hamlet and tell my people about God. We have many problems and needs here. We have had many young people commit suicide. Please, I will give you this Complex Center free of charge to hold public meetings if you will come back and tell us about God." We knew immediately that God wanted us to return to conduct a series of evangelistic meetings. We told him we would give him an answer before flying back home in the next two days.

After praying about this and counselling with some local individuals it was clear the Lord presented us with a Macedonian call so to speak. We met with the mayor and set some tentative dates and upon our return home we received permission from our leaders to pursue this clear invitation.

We contacted the mayor and confirmed the dates. However, these dates would not work in conjunction with the student ministry which was a set time each year. So, we planned a five-day evangelistic campaign with a focus on reaching all ages of the Hamlet. Once again, we sought and received permission from our leadership.

252

IN THE WAR

We secured and brought special music from the Winnipeg area which helped to draw people out each evening.

The campaign took place in March of 2013. Trudy and I had arrived a couple days early just to make sure things were in place. Unexpectantly I was immediately hit with an unusual illness that turned into a horrendous and dreadful cough. We knew this was a direct attack from the enemy. Consequently, we surmised God had great plans for these dear people. We prayed much but the illness prevailed throughout the entire campaign. This coughing kept me up most every night. Every night I would make my way downstairs to the couch and attempt to sleep sitting up. Sitting up seemed the only way to stop the coughing. We preached the gospel for five nights in the Complex Center. Each night the Lord gave me His anointing and blessing, and I was able to preach without coughing and I preached with authority and power from the Holy Spirit. Upon the completion of each message, I would extend a public invitation for any who wanted to repent of sin and receive Christ to come forward and pray with me. I would always say, "Remember, if you come forward you are publicly admitting you need to repent and receive Christ as your Lord and Savior."

By the end of the fifth night, we had witnessed a total of 248 people walk forward to receive Christ. An average of 50 people of all ages walked forward per night. All glory to God. Once I prayed with them, I would conduct a brief basic follow-up containing pertinent information. Once I finished with this, they were escorted to an area to record their names, addresses, and telephone numbers and to receive Bibles and basic follow-up materials. All the recorded information was given to church leaders to continue with the important follow-up after we had gone.

During the day it was not uncommon for us to have several visitors who had received Christ the night before seeking counsel regarding their new relationship with Christ. Some also came

253

seeking to repent and receive Christ. Over coffee we would bow together, and they would invite Jesus to come into their heart.

The men who came and provided special music for the campaign confessed they did not expect to witness what they witnessed. They admitted that on the first night while I was preaching, they stood in the back of the auditorium with their arms folded and kept saying to each other "no one will respond…no one is going to go forward." They admitted that they were astonished when 50 people got up and humbly walked forward in repentance. They also admitted they were ashamed, and the Lord had lovingly rebuked them. One said, "I have never witnessed anything like this." I told them that, "God will show up in some of the most unlikely places in the world if He is truly invited." They agreed.

Plane to the Arctic

IN THE WAR

Cutting the Ribbon Ceremony in the Arctic

Audience listening to preaching

Trudy preaching in the Arctic

Chapter 35

TENSIONS ARISE

Our team came home excited about what God had done in that remote arctic Hamlet. We were frankly surprised at the response of our church which at the time had no pastor and frankly were sliding into a very liberal state theologically. One leader approached me after our friends who provided the music for the recent campaign gave a report in our church. He said, "Bob, now not to minimize, but do you think those 248 people came forward because they want what you have?" When I questioned him further, I discovered he meant that perhaps they came forward with the hopes of obtaining material things rather than to receive Christ.

As we talked with others over the next few days it became clear to us that truthfully, and sadly, many did not believe that those who came forward in our campaign came forward to receive Christ.

Shockingly, one highly educated individual who held prominent position in a Bible school suggested that to ask people to come forward is making it too easy for them. He recommended that I should ask them to raise their hands instead. Of course, we had experienced these kinds of comments before, but it was still disappointing to hear their disbelief.

More disappointment came during a conference out east with our mission. Before leaving the conference, we were informed we

BOB MCLAUGHLIN

had a new Mobilization Director. I asked the Canadian Director if this new man had been briefed with regard to the special assignment we had with the northern ministry leadership and himself. He said, "I have told him that you will comply 100 percent with all he instructs you to do." I responded with, "yes of course, but I'm asking if you have informed him of the special arrangement and agreement we have with regards to the northern ministry?" Sadly, at this point his face took on a stern look and squaring his jaw as well he said, "I have informed him you will comply 100 percent with all he instructs you to do." Realizing it was fruitless to continue I simply thanked him and did not pursue it further.

We continued attending mission conferences and had hoped to be going to some 70 churches as well. The list of these 70 churches were sent to us several months earlier by our director, however he informed us we could not go to any churches until he gave us his permission. So, we continued recruiting students to be involved in the annual arctic ministry.

Things intensified as this arctic ministry began to expand with the endorsement of the Bishop of the Arctic Dieses. During a meeting with the Bishop in Yellowknife, NWT, he personally extended an invitation to us to bring the gospel to 33 villages under his authority, with the understanding that we would come alongside the 33 Anglican churches that were currently without an Anglican priest and work hand in hand with them in preaching the Gospel. These villages were spread across thousands of miles in the vast sparsely populated arctic.

Anyone who has ever travelled to the Arctic knows that it is extremely expensive to minister there. A commercial flight can cost twice the amount for a flight to Europe. If one is forced to rent a hotel room for lack of billeting the accommodations in the Arctic can be as much as $250 per bed per night, even if you shared a room. Food is also awfully expensive.

IN THE WAR

For a few years this arctic ministry in conjunction with the Bible college went well. But tensions with our Canadian leadership escalated. It seemed nothing we did met their approval. Thus, the successful arctic ministry continued to receive a cold shoulder.

Chapter 36

THE PROPOSALS

As tensions continued, we were feeling more and more caught in the middle. However, we were confident that our God was not only aware but that He was leading and preparing the way forward. We knew He would work all things out for good. However, the way forward was not as smooth as we would have liked, but we persevered.

While on another trip north, Trudy and I were having lunch with some dear friends in Alaska. This couple had been our friends for many years. They were also aware of the situation we were involved in. Though currently retired, they had served many years as missionaries and were highly respected. They had served in both Alaska and Canada.

As we finished lunch our trusted friend told us, "I have a surprise for you two today. There is someone I want you to meet. In fact, he is flying in today from the interior just so he can meet the two of you." We were shocked when he told us who this man was. This man too had served with them in the same mission for many years in both Alaska and Russia. He was retired as well but active in another ministry he founded training pilots.

To our great surprise our friend then announced that he had drafted a proposal and emailed it to our Canadian Director.

I questioned, "what kind of proposal did you send?" He said his friend the pilot had mentioned that there are 500 villages in Siberia, Russia, with populations between 1,000 to 3,000 each which have never been reached with the Gospel. This proposal suggests a joint venture agreement between the Canadian mission, the northern mission, and the mission headed up by the founder of the pilot training mission. The proposal suggested that the mission would free us up to conduct evangelistic campaigns throughout the entire region in all 500 villages of Siberia.

We were beside ourselves. We could not believe our ears. Our hopes ran high with excitement. These two highly qualified men (though retired) were still respected within missionary circles. After all, they both possessed an amazing legacy. Their names in the mission were synonymous with unconventional, Godfearing, cutting-edge, fearless leaders whose mission it was to lead people in getting the job done. I thought surely if they believe God could use us as evangelists for such a huge task, that leadership would endorse the proposal.

An hour or so later we were standing around our friends' dining room table looking on as the man of the hour watched a video of one of our evangelistic meetings in Kugluktuk, NU. He was pleased with the video and said, "Let me show you where I think we can work together to reach thousands of people who have yet to hear the Gospel." With that he laid out a huge map of Siberia and continued explaining how he felt we could be used of God in this way.

Our unexpected meeting lasted a couple of hours and ended in prayer together, asking for God's blessing on this possible joint venture. Before we drove him back to the airport, we made tentative plans to travel to Siberia together in the future, pending the approval of the proposal by the current mission's leadership.

It had become clear to us that these men recognized our gifts and felt the mission would benefit by allowing us to use these gifts in assisting the Russian mission and expanding the ministry by

IN THE WAR

reaching these unreached villages in Siberia. Admittedly we hoped this proposal would not only be approved but would launch us into a better fit in the mission using the God given gift of evangelism.

In the last few months prior to this proposal, we found ourselves questioning our calling. Though we were faithful in performing our duties as mobilizers for the mission, there appeared to be little fruit for our labor. Try as we may our work seemed to lack leadership approval.

Sadly, the proposal was not approved. Furthermore, the leadership accused us of potentially tarnishing the reputation and legacy of these two highly respected men. Though we were disappointed, we continued to do the best we could with our responsibilities. However, we sensed the Lord was about to do a major change in our ministry.

We had noticed that we were no longer invited to attend the large mission conferences across Canada like we were in the early days. The new director of mobilization seemed to want to distance himself from us. This became very evident during the last conference where we represented the mission. No matter how many times we tried to discuss the obvious tension between us, he would refuse to discuss it.

Eventually, I came right out and asked him why he was treating us this way. In anger he said, "I'm just doing what our director told me to do." Wow! There it was. On the last day of that conference, God provided a prophetic word for us.

The mission display table beside ours was manned by a wonderful husband-and-wife team representing their African mission. For the last three years, we had our tables side by side and had developed a wonderful relationship with these missionaries.

As the conference was coming to an end, and before we began to tear down our display table, our friend with the African mission approached us and asked if he could share a concern he had. We responded with, "Absolutely. Please, what is it you want to tell us?"

He quickly scanned all around making sure our new director was not present. When he was sure of this he said, "Bob and Trudy, we held a special prayer meeting last night for you." He continued, "We have witnessed the way you have been treated by your director and after we prayed, God gave me a word for you two." I said, "Okay, what is it He wants you to tell us?" He looked us in the eyes and said, "You guys will not be here next year." He finished with, "I'm sorry but that's what God wanted me to tell you." I responded with, "Thank you, we think you are right." Before leaving he said, "We really feel terrible about what we witnessed."

We went home and fell to our knees and cried out to God again. We asked Him to help us navigate through this difficult situation. God answered our prayers. We continued our work but with a heavy heart.

Several months earlier the Canadian director sent us a list of 70 churches he wanted us to contact with the plan of mobilizing resources and potential future missionaries. However, he informed us we were not to contact any until he gave us the green light. It was frustrating, but we continued as best we could.

I knew our work was sadly suspect when our Canadian director demanded we begin producing a weekly report of our activities including almost an hourly account of our work each day. We complied but we knew it was a downward slope from here on out. After all, all the other mobilizers were required to provide a monthly report only.

After counselling with some trusted dear friends, we decided to risk making our own proposal. After much prayer, we drafted what we thought was a logical proposal. In essence we asked to be removed from the mobilization department and placed under the special ministry's category. We suggested we could be used as evangelists in assisting the mission's missionaries all over the world. We also offered to do all the fund raising necessary for such

264

IN THE WAR

a ministry. We sent the proposal to the mission's board of directors as well as our leaders.

In response, the Canadian Director told us he would pray about it and most likely would check with all area directors. The area director of Alaska responded immediately and sent the Canadian director an email and copied us as well stating that he and the northern ministry could use us as much as four times a year in this type of ministry. Meanwhile, our director now informed us we could contact the 70 churches he had made us wait on all these months.

Within a couple of weeks, our Canadian Director Skyped us with his decision. He told us all the area directors around the world informed him they could not or would not use our evangelism gifts to assist them in conducting evangelism in their areas of mission. It seems he did not realize we had been copied on the email he received from the Alaskan director. He also told us that because of the response he received, he has decided to say a firm no to the proposal we presented. What he said next, we suspected was coming.

"Bob and Trudy, now that you know that there is no place in our worldwide mission where you can be used as evangelists, I am recommending you resign from our mission immediately."

I said, "Okay, we will." At that he said, "Praise God. You have made the right decision." He continued, "we will help you transition out and I will expect your written resignation within a few days."

Within a few days we transitioned out of that mission organization and immediately joined the mission we are currently with.

International Christian Mission Services has been raised up by God to accommodate people called by God to conduct a particular ministry based on the individual's supernatural, Holy Ghost endowed gifts. At the time of this writing there are currently 76 agencies around the world serving under ICMS. Our agency is called Salvation Today Ministries.

265

BOB MCLAUGHLIN

Over the last seven years we have preached the gospel face-to-face with hundreds of thousands of people all over the world and tens of thousands have repented and given their lives to Christ. We give all the glory and honor and praise to God.

PART EIGHT
TRIALS AND TRIBULATIONS CONTINUE

Chapter 37

Another New Ministry: Salvation Today Ministries

The Psalmist proclaimed, *"I will instruct you and teach you in the way which you should go; I will counsel you with My eye upon you."* Psalm 32:8 (NASB) Also, *"Delight yourself in the LORD; and He will give you the desires of your heart, commit your way to the LORD, trust also in Him, and He will do it."* Psalm 37:4-5 (NASB)

As mentioned in the previous chapter, our proposal to be used as evangelists was rejected by the Canadian Director of the mission we were serving with at the time. According to him, all area directors from around the world responded negatively to his inquiry if they could use us as evangelists in assisting them in reaching people with the gospel. However, for reasons known only to him and God, he clearly ignored the Area Director of the Northern ministry who stated in an email to him and to us that he could use us as much as four times a year.

How often would I say during those trying and difficult days, "All I ever wanted to do was preach the gospel to as many people as possible in my lifetime." This has always been my true heart's desire. Personally, I really have no other desire in life. I just want to preach the gospel, and in doing so we will be obedient to our gifts and ultimately our calling.

BOB MCLAUGHLIN

Truth be told, we had sensed that our proposal would be rejected by the Canadian Director. We knew there was no way he was going to accept it. Thus, while we awaited his so-called investigation to see if any of the area directors would or could use us as evangelists, we began looking for an organization that truly allows ones supernatural Holy Ghost endowed gift to be used to the fullest.

It was at this point that God raised up a friend who was aware of our search and he provided us with contact information with a global ministry called International Christian Mission Services. Once we were forced to resign from the large mission, we had served with for the last four and a half years, we quickly applied to ICMS. Not long after we were officially accepted as an independent agency and Salvation Today Ministries was born.

As we thought of what to name our new ministry, we sought the Lord's guidance through prayer. Again and again, He reminded us of an urgency within our hearts to preach this gospel to as many people as possible for the remainder of our lives. At this point He reminded me that though He is patient, He is not willing that any should perish but for all to come to repentance. (2 Peter 3:9b) As humans, we find it somewhat difficult to have patience about a certain thing and to have an urgency regarding the same issue at the same time. However, because God is God, He can have patience and urgency all at the same time and with equal intensity. We read about His urgency for people to come to Him in 2 Corinthians 6:2b," *behold now is "THE ACCEPTABLE TIME, now is "THE DAY OF SALVATION"* (NASB). Thus, Salvation Today Ministries was born.

Once we were fully and legally organized, we began preaching the gospel in the Philippines and countries in Africa. Arctic ministry continued for a while but as mentioned in a previous chapter, the Lord allowed it to be shut down.

Trudy and I knew that the Lord would open a way for us to use our gifts and our calling. STM has clearly been that way forward. The results of our obedience to the prompting of the Holy Spirit

IN THE WAR

in resigning from the former mission and to form and begin a new evangelistic ministry has been nothing short of miraculous.

Salvation Today Ministries in corporation with other evangelistic ministries has been clearly used of God to accomplish the following results. From the beginning of 2015 and through January of 2020, Trudy and I had preached a total of 1,451 evangelistic sermons face-to-face with an estimated combined audience of half a million people. In those evangelistic sermons, we have witnessed just under 424,000 publicly indicated decisions for Christ. ALL GLORY BE TO GOD!

These kinds of statistics admittedly can be rather difficult for many people in the North American church to grasp and believe. So, many find it easier to disbelieve it. Yet their inability to grasp and believe what God is doing has no bearing on the reality of what He has done. Sadly, that disbelief robs God of His right to be praised and glorified for it.

Upon the completion of every evangelistic campaign we are privileged to be involved in, we must pause and remember the words of our Lord Jesus, *"I am the vine, you are the branches; he who abides in Me and I in him, he bears much fruit, for apart from Me you can do nothing."* John 15:5 (NASB).

So, as opposition continues, hundreds of thousands are coming to Christ. God has counseled us with His eye upon us, and He has given us the desires of our heart as promised, and we believe He will continue to do just that. We continue to trust Him to allow us to preach the gospel with urgency to as many people as possible for the remainder of our lives.

Preaching in Africa

Trudy preaching in Africa

IN THE WAR

Preaching in Africa

Chapter 38

YOU DON'T FIT THE MISSIONARY PROFILE

In August of 1980, Trudy, and I, along with our four children, James, Joshua, Priscilla, and Rebekah, arrived in British Columbia, following our long 3,200-mile journey by automobile across the continent. We were excited to begin our new ministry in Canada. As mentioned in a previous chapter, we had spent our first two years in full time ministry in Fairfax, Virginia.

In those early days of ministry, we were supported by several churches in central New Hampshire. Before our move to Fairfax, VA, the pastors of these churches followed the biblical example of sending us out as missionaries in a beautiful commissioning service in 1978.

Once we got settled in our new home, we immediately began looking for a church where we could become members and enjoy worship and fellowship with new friends in the area. Eventually, we found a church we felt attracted to. Over time that church began supporting our ministry.

With every move we made over the years, this was our habit. We would seek fellowship and membership with a local church. We were always so thankful for the support we received from these churches and individuals. However, we noticed over time we began

BOB MCLAUGHLIN

losing support, especially when we began our own evangelistic ministry in 1986 in obedience to the calling and gifting as an itinerant evangelist.

We always took seriously the command of Jesus to, *"Go into all the world and preach the gospel to all creation."* Mark 16:15 (NASB) Our new evangelistic ministry put us in front of thousands of people all over the world. At first, we were able to conduct many crusades both in the United States and Canada. However, there came a shift in the overall methodology of evangelistic thinking in the evangelical church. And sadly, the genuinely gifted evangelists were no longer being used in reaching communities in North America like they were in the past.

Thankfully, the Billy Graham Evangelistic Association years before realised this shift and began conducting huge conferences for the itinerant evangelists. These conferences drew thousands of lesser-known evangelists from all over the world and encouraged them to go to the harvest fields of the world with the life-changing Gospel.

As a result of this shift, God has taken these evangelists to be used all over the world. Our own ministry went from conducting small crusades in the US and Canada to large evangelistic meetings in Africa and Asia, and the former Soviet Union.

However, our ministry as an itinerant evangelist for reasons known only to God is not viewed in the same way as missionaries. The following is a classic example of this truth.

Trudy and I were attending a large church in Winnipeg, Manitoba, a few years ago. We were enjoying the fellowship and the solid preaching brought forth by the pastor. This church had a large section displayed on a wall with pictures of all the missionaries it supported. In the middle of all those pictures was a picture frame with the words "This could be you." As we would pass this wall, we often thought how good it would be to have a church of this size take us on as part of their mission program. However,

276

IN THE WAR

we deliberately chose not to seek that possibility ourselves. We strongly believed if God wanted them to support us, He would have the church approach us.

Every Sunday when we were not traveling internationally, we would travel into the city to attend our home church. One Sunday, unsolicited, we were approached by friends. The husband was on staff with the church, working in their office. He said to us that morning, "There are several returning missionaries that our church has been supporting. Many of them are not returning to the mission field. There are about five openings available for support. We want to introduce you to the chairman of the missions committee and encourage you to apply for support." Trudy and I looked at each other knowing that God had orchestrated this moment.

Our friends led us to the chairman and introduced us. Following the warm and cordial introductions, they said to him, "Bob and Trudy's ministry should be considered for support of our church. The chairman agreed and told us that there would be funds available if we would be approved by the committee. He took our information and told us we should fill out an application as soon as possible, emphasising that there would be five openings for potential support.

We did as we were instructed and with excitement filled out the necessary application forms and submitted them to the missions committee. Frankly, I must admit I was sure that this church would accept us and support our ministry. After all they approached us with this possibility.

A few weeks later, we were approached by the chairman of the missions committee with an invitation to meet with the mission's board for a formal interview. The interview took place in the home of one of the committee members. The meeting opened in prayer and commenced with the usual kind of questions. They thanked us for coming and informed us we would hear from them soon.

Several weeks passed and we had not heard from the missions committee. Our ministry's board meetings were coming soon, and we thought it would be good to inform them of the church's decision. I telephoned the chairman informing him that our meeting was approaching, and we were wondering if the missions committee had made their decision. He replied that a decision has been made and a letter was being drafted and will be mailed to us. I asked if he could tell me over the phone what they had decided.

I admit I was unusually hopeful that the answer would be a resounding yes. That hope was immediately dashed when he said, "Bob, I am sorry to say that we as a committee decided your application is rejected. You will not be supported by our church as missionaries." I was silent for a moment before asking, "Could you please tell me why we have been rejected?" He simply said, "You don't fit the missionary profile."

Though we were disappointed, we continued attending the church. One Sunday morning I saw the chairman and approached him and thanked him for considering us for support. I also mentioned that we do not fully understand why we were rejected but that we do respect their decision. I then asked him the following: I mentioned that we need prayer and asked if the church could at least pray for us and our evangelistic ministry. He said, "Bob, yes of course it's the least we could do for you and Trudy." I assured him he could follow our itinerary with our newsletters and the church could pray for our campaigns. He agreed.

Over the next few months as each campaign approached, we expected the church would announce it and pray for us. When we did not hear any prayers for our ministry, we desired to think the best and assumed they were praying for us while we were away conducting the actual international campaigns. With this in mind, we approached some friends and asked them if our campaigns were being prayed for by the church when we were preaching overseas. We were sorely disappointed when they informed us that the

IN THE WAR

church was not being made aware of our ministry and there were no prayers on our behalf as promised.

I lovingly confronted the chairman about his promise. He sheepishly apologized, admitting he did not follow through with his promise. Trudy and I decided to look for a different church with the hopes of finding one that would at least pray for us as we obey the command to preach the Gospel. We decided to just continue our evangelistic ministry. We also firmly believe that we are obeying the great commission even though they tell us boldly "You do not fit the missionary profile."

Chapter 39

HE'S A CULT-LIKE SPEAKER. PEOPLE RESPOND TO HIM, NOT GOD.

One definition of the word cult is: a misplaced or excessive admiration for a particular person or thing. "a cult of personality surrounding the leaders."

During a lunch meeting with my pastor, he commented, "Bob, I have heard some amazing stories of the morning chapel service at the Christian high school where you recently preached. I was told that most everyone considered it a mini revival meeting." I responded, "Yes, it was truly an amazing service." I continued, "Pastor, that service was electric with the awesome power of the Holy Spirit. When I gave the invitation to repent and come forward, within moments over 80% of those present came forward, filling the front and the isles to the point where there was no more room to come forward. Many simply knelt where they were and repented. Many students were in tears. It was truly a God thing."

My pastor said, "Yes, that's what I heard as well, but sadly it seems not all believe it was a work of God." I responded with surprise, "Really?" He continued, "Yes. In fact, I was talking with the youth coordinator, a staff member at the high school, about that chapel service. "He continued, "I told him that I had heard it was a revival, and that I wondered what his opinion was. Bob, he said it depends on who you talk to." I questioned him further saying, "Just what do you mean?" He said the youth coordinator said with a smirk, "Bob is a cult like speaker/figure and that people respond to Bob, not to God."

Once again, I was devastated that someone would question my preaching to the point of making such an accusation. I also believed that though this comment was intended to hurt me, it was more of an insult toward God and was also further confirmation of our calling.

To be accused of being a cult like leader was truly humiliating. I remember as a student in Bible college studying the subject of cults and their leaders. I was always fascinated yet very disturbed with the sad reality of how a person could deceive people to believe a particular way, even if it were clearly contrary to all they had been taught, and to follow them to the point of even self destruction. One sad case was the Reverend Jim Jones who led over 800 men women and children to take their own lives by drinking cool aid with poison. Of course, there are many more documented stories of such religious leaders and the tragedies they brought upon human lives. The enemy of God, Satan, delights in causing confusion and deception. Satan enjoys destroying people's faith. We read about this deception in the words of Jesus in John 10:10, *"The thief comes only to steal and kill and destroy..."* (NASB)

Many cults tend to have a smattering of similarities to Judeo Christian religion, which can easily deceive people into believing they are simply following a different type of leader with more of a charismatic flavor that appeals to their emotions and feelings.

As an evangelist, a preacher of the gospel of Jesus Christ, I have always been amazed at how God would take a simple message and use it to draw people to Himself. I was also very aware that truthfully, even though it was my voice people heard during the message, ultimately it was the Holy Spirit who drew people to

IN THE WAR

Himself. Because I was aware of this very fact, I wanted people to fully understand that they were coming to Christ and not to me. I would always include this in every public invitation I gave.

People who come to Christ under our evangelistic ministry have always been instructed in our follow-up to follow Christ as their Lord and Savior. Never have they been instructed to follow a man. In hindsight, I'm astonished as to the many Christians that are deceived to believe a lie. And in this case seek to minimize an amazing movement of God's Holy Spirit. Over the years I have been called many things, but this truly smacked of a genuine insult.

So, as we persevere in the ministry, we know that opposition will always be a part of anything that will help people have an intimate and personal relationship with their creator. Those who are successful in helping to fulfill the command of Jesus to *"Go into all the world and preach the gospel to all creation"* Mark 16:15 (NASB) must come face-to-face with this reality.

Jesus said, *"Blessed are you when people insult you and persecute you, and falsely say all kinds of evil against you because of Me. Rejoice and be glad, for your reward in heaven is great; for in the same way, they persecuted the prophets who were before you."* Mathew 5:11-12 (NASB) Thus we are in good company.

Chapter 40

WHAT YOU'RE DOING IS DANGEROUS FOR THOSE YOU PREACH TO

Oswald Sanders said, "The frontiers of the kingdom of God were never advanced by men and women of caution."

George Patton said, "Every mistake in war is excusable except for two: inactivity and a refusal to take a risk. These two mistakes will cost you the war..."

As I have said numerous times in the pages of this book, we are involved in an intense spiritual warfare. This battle, sadly, also involves opposition from within the body of Christ.

I am determined to overcome opposition of mere human beings to accomplish with obedience my high calling of almighty God.

When opposition comes, I remember the words of the old missionary who said to me, "That's of God, young man! That's of God!" You may recall he said those words to me in response to what God had said to me while I was in prayer as a young Christian. He said, "I'm going to use you in a powerful and mighty way... but not without a lot of trials and tribulations!" Now the title of this chapter stems from the following.

Some friends and supporters offered to open their home for us to hold a Salvation Today Ministries informational and casual evening. The meeting was open to all people from their church, which at the time had no pastor. We knew there were many in that church who were not supportive of us in general. We were informed that we were too evangelical for them. We assumed those people would not bother to come to this prearranged meeting.

Unfortunately, this church was the product of a church split. Without pastoral leadership, the church was sliding theologically to the left and liberalism, but there were still a good number of people holding to the evangelical slant.

The meeting was attended by about 20 people. To our surprise, a couple who had made no bones about their disdain for us chose to come and take front and center seats where all in attendance could see them. Everyone knew this couple's dislike for us. Everyone also knew this couple were in control of that church.

Our hosts thanked everyone for coming and opened in prayer before introducing us. I stood and opened the Word of God to read a passage of scripture. I said, "I would like to begin with the reading of God's word". At this point the wife of the couple shifted her body around on her seat and throwing her head slightly back she rolled her eyes and scoffed. Everyone witnessed this. I knew at that moment we were in for a rough evening.

We shared a video of one of our Arctic campaigns and spent a few minutes explaining our evangelistic ministry. After several minutes we offered to answer any questions that they may have.

The first question was regarding the follow up of our evangelistic campaigns. The person asked, "Who is responsible for the follow up after your campaign is over?" I simply shared that once I finished preaching, a national pastor would conduct the immediate follow up for all those who received Christ and that the local churches were responsible for the follow up. I also emphasized that as an evangelist my responsibility is the preaching of the gospel, calling people to repentance and inviting them to receive Christ as Lord and Savior.

IN THE WAR

The follow up question continued and no matter how many times I informed them the follow up is the responsibility of the area churches, it was clearly unacceptable to them. They felt I was being irresponsible.

Next, someone asked if I had ever preached in a remote village where there are no churches. I answered with a firm yes. I said, "I have done this in the past and will in the future." It became clear that question was a set up because they then called upon a retired missionary who had faithfully ministered in an African country for 30 years to address my answer. They asked her what her opinion was of my insistence on preaching the gospel in remote villages where there are no churches to deal with the follow up.

She responded with the following. "Well, it is dangerous for those you preach to who live in remote villages. They need proper follow up and without it, they can't grow in their faith."

Someone then said, "You need to listen to her. She has 30 years' experience in Africa. She knows what she's talking about." I responded with the following.

I said, "I would rather preach the good news in a remote village, giving them opportunity to receive Jesus and secure their salvation, than for them to never hear the gospel preached and die and go to hell! How is that wrong?" I told them, "The thief on the cross had no follow up and was never baptised yet Jesus said to him, 'This day you will be with me in paradise.'" I also emphasised the fact that the Holy Spirit is more than capable of doing the follow up.

Eventually, one person came to our defence and said, "I don't believe you people! This couple wants to go out into the world preaching the gospel and all you do is attack them with this whole thing about follow up. They have explained fully their stand on this issue. We should rally behind them with support."

The meeting ended at this point. Refreshments were served but many left without the fellowship. We had instructed them that if they were interested in our ministry to sign the sign-up sheet on the table. Sadly, only one person signed the sheet.

I am reminded of a passage of scripture that relates to the encounter we experienced that evening. We read in Mark 9:39 where John, a disciple of Jesus, noticed someone that was not part of "their team" casting out demons. John told Jesus that *"... we tried to prevent him because he was not following us."* Jesus said, *"Do not hinder him..."* and in verse 40 Jesus continued with, *"For he who is not against us is for us."* (NASB)

Unfortunately, we continue receiving opposition regarding follow up.

Preaching in remote African village

Chapter 41

WE DON'T BELIEVE YOUR NUMBERS

"For those who believe, no proof is necessary. For those who do not believe, no proof is possible." This quote by the late and famous economist Stuart Chase rang true to me shortly after an uncomfortable but necessary confrontation with a wealthy businessperson.

Sadly, we had a falling out with him. For a few months, we had made several failed attempts to invite him and his wife for dinner and have an "all cards on the table" discussion. Our hope and sincere intention were to resolve the strained relationship and restore us back to the warm Christian fellowship we once enjoyed. Eventually they responded with a negative email implying they found it interesting that we would want to get together after I had sent him a rather blunt email. We counselled with several friends as to what they thought we should do. They suggested we try one more time to invite them to dinner at our home.

We did, and to our surprise they agreed to come for dinner. I am sure they were rather reluctant with this decision.

The dinner, though a bit awkward, managed to have some causal but cautious conversation. Following this uncomfortable dinner, we retired to our living-room to have our talk.

We began by apologizing for the blunt email I had sent to him. This email was in response to several times in which he had spoken to me in a rather harsh tone.

Following this necessary apology, I walked them through the history of our relationship with them and the organization we had resigned from. This organization, as mentioned in an earlier chapter, refused to allow us any practical way to remain on staff, thus forcing us to resign to use the gifting given by God more effectively. However, our guests were not pleased that we would leave this organization. As we walked them through those four and a half years, we thought that surely they would understand and recognize that we were in essence forced to resign. We also had hoped they would apologize to us as well, and our relationship would be restored. Sadly, and to our great disappointment, the meeting went south. He responded by saying, "We do not believe your numbers." He was referring to the reports we give in our newsletters. These reports were the statistics recorded by our national team in each evangelistic meeting of all who publicly showed they repented and received Christ. He also said that people were mocking us with comments like, "If there were only 2 or 3 more Bobs, we could win the world to Christ in no time." So sad. Perhaps they forgot about Jonah's preaching in Nineveh, where the entire city of 120,000 people repented, including the King.

At this point I said, "We never called those statistics 'Converts.'" I continued, "we always call them publicly indicated decisions for Christ." He responded saying, "We refuse to believe your stats.

I knew at this point there was little hope humanly speaking of restoring this fractured relationship. After a few more minutes of his disapproval of us and our ministry, he stood and said, "Well it's time for us to go." At that moment I realized the olive branch we had extended lay crushed on our carpet. They left our home and to this day we have not had any fellowship with them. The sweet fellowship we once enjoyed is gone...for now. Only our God can restore that which we once enjoyed.

IN THE WAR

Preaching in the Philippines

Trudy preaching to huge crowd in Philippines

Preaching in the Philippines

Bob preaching to 12,000 high school students

IN THE WAR

Bob preaching to huge high school in Africa

Chapter 42

DESPITE CONTINUED TRIALS AND TRIBULATIONS, WE MOVE FORWARD VICTORIOUSLY INTO THE BATTLE

Yes, the intense spiritual battle continues and will continue for the rest of our lives. The entire human race cannot escape this battle. The enemy of God, Satan, and his army of demons are fighting and will continue despite the fact they know they will lose this battle and eventually be thrown into the flaming bowels of hell.

We read about this intense battle in the book of Ephesians. The Apostle Paul wrote to the church in Ephesus, *"Finally, be strong in the Lord and in the strength of His might. Put on the full armor of God, so that you will be able to stand firm against the schemes of the devil. For our struggle is not against flesh and blood, but against the rulers against the powers, against the world forces of this darkness, against the spiritual forces of wickedness in the heavenly places."* Ephesians 6:10-12 (NASB)

Yes, there is no question that these enemies of God can be terrifying and clearly a formidable foe. However, we need not allow fear to overcome us. Why, you ask? Because God has provided for all His children the necessary spiritual armor we need as we engage in this spiritual warfare. The Bible calls it the "full armor of God."

This armor consists of six critical components that the Apostle describes in Ephesian 6:14-17.

First, we are to GIRD OUR LOINS WITH TRUTH. Next, we are to put on the BREST PLATE OF RIGHTEOUSNESS. Third, we are to shod our feet with the GOSPEL OF PEACE. Fourth, we are to hold the shield of FAITH. Fifth, we are to put on the helmet of SALVATION. And finally, sixth, we are to have the sword of the Spirit THE WORD OF GOD. If we put on this full armor, we can endure the battle. If not, we will indeed lose the battle.

So, as we live our lives from day to day, if we keep the full amor of God on, this will keep us from losing this intense battle. Now, that is not to say we will not encounter ongoing intense trials and tribulations. This is just a fact of life. Some attacks can and will knock us off our feet. At times we will even think we cannot get back up. However, if you took the time to read this entire book, you know that in my case I was knocked on my back numerous times. In fact, I truly believe the enemy thought he had defeated me. His desire was and still is to kill me. The enemy was wrong, and this book is evidence of that fact.

Friend if you are a Christian and have been living in sin and feel there is absolutely no way you can be restored and forgiven for that which you have done, you are wrong, and the enemy is delighted you feel defeated. It matters not what you have done. Forgiveness can be yours if you will simply fall on your face before God and repent, confessing your sin. Repentance is a change of mind and a change of heart and involves action. The action point for you is to turn from your sin back to the Lord.

If you have given your heart to God, I assure you that you are a child of God and on the authority of Him alone He will move heaven and earth to reach down and help His child and pull you back onto your feet. Too often the enemy convinces believers who have fallen into sin that there's no way God can forgive them. They feel they have sinned so badly that forgiveness is out of their reach. They

IN THE WAR

feel they can never be restored, and they feel that even God cannot rescue them. I felt like that when I fell into sin. But the truth is you cannot fall so far that God's gracious hand cannot grasp your hand and pull you out of the slippery mess you entered because of sin.

Allow me to help you understand this by using a simple illustration. Picture in your mind a huge bowl the size of a stadium. Now picture yourself walking around the top edge of this bowl. As you walk around the top, you have been made aware that the entire inside of this huge bowl has been greased from top to bottom. At this point the thought enters your mind that it would be fun to slide down into that huge bowl. Even if reason dawns on your thinking that it will be difficult to get out of this slippery bowl, the temptation to experience this exciting and exhilarating slide of a lifetime overwhelms you and reason slips out of your mind.

So you take the plunge. The slide is more than you could ever have imagined. The speed thrills you, causing your flesh to tingle. You slide hundreds of feet to the bottom with breakneck speed which allows your body to continue up the other side. You note that you almost reach the top of the other side as you slow to a complete stop. Then you begin another slide only this time you are sliding back down the path you slid up on. The thrill continues but with less intensity as you continue to slide down one side and up the other. Eventually the momentum weakens, and each slide up does not bring you as high up as the previous slide.

For a pittance of pleasure, you now discover that this thrill ride like all sin ends only one way. You eventually end up sitting at the bottom. The ride is finished. The adrenaline begins to wear off. And the thrill has worn off. You sit motionless. As you sit catching your breath a horrifying reality begins to wash over you like a tsunami. You ask yourself, how am I going to get out of here? Try as you may, your feet can't find any traction. With each attempt to scale the greased wall you slip and fall and slide and return to the bottom defeated and exhausted. Any hope you may have attempted

BOB MCLAUGHLIN

to muster has now evaporated. Your shout for help is heard only by you. There is no one who can reach you and help pull you out.

What's needed at this desperate point is a miracle! Only God can perform miracles. Only He can extend His hand and pull you up and out. But for this to happen, you must call on Him. To do so you must be willing to admit your sin. Confess that sin to Him and tell Him that you are sorry for deliberately taking that foolish thrill slide. Ask Him to forgive you and to help you to not go back to that thrill slide again. If you are willing to confess your sin, He will forgive you and restore you and cleanse you from your sin through the shed blood of Jesus. The Bible says, *"If we confess our sin, He is faithful and righteous to forgive us our sins and to cleanse us from all unrighteousness."* 1 John 1:9 (NASB)

What's happening in your life? Is your marriage in turmoil? Do you have sexual problems? Do you have a drinking problem? Do you have a drug problem? Do you have anger issues? Have you even contemplated ending your life? Are you in prison? Have you lost your family? What sin has brought you to the messy bottom of despair? There is nothing you have done that God cannot forgive.

Please allow me to lead you in a prayer. Are you ready to turn back to the Lord? If so, pray this prayer right now, right where you are. Say, Dear God, I have sinned against you. I have made a mess of my life, and I am in desperate need of your gracious help. Please forgive me for all my deliberate and willful sin against you. Cleanse me and restore me to a right relationship with you. Help me to allow You to be Lord of my life. Thank you, Jesus. Amen.

Now perhaps some of you as you read this realize that you have never surrendered your life to Christ. This should cause you great concern. For you see according to the Word of God, the Bible, either you belong to God, or you belong to Satan.

The Bible clearly points this out in the book of Ephesians 2:1-2 *"And you were dead in your trespasses and sins, in which you formally walked according to the course of this world, according to the prince*

IN THE WAR

of the power of the air, of the spirit that is now working in the sons of disobedience. Among them we too all formerly lived in the lust of our flesh, indulging the desires of the flesh and of the mind, and were by nature children of wrath, even as the rest." (NASB) The prince mentioned here is the devil.

As you ponder this you may even protest saying, "Are we not all children of God? That thought has been proclaimed down through the centuries." Well, the enemy delights in this type of wishful thinking. However, no matter how boldly this thinking is proclaimed, it has no biblical foundation.

Let me explain. We must understand that yes, we are all God's creation. This is indeed a fact. God in His infinite wisdom knit your flesh and bone together in your mother's womb and allowed you to take your first breath when you were born. But that in and of itself does not make you His child. You are simply His creation. Because of the fall of Adam and Eve, we by nature are born in sin and consequently are children of wrath and the devil, Satan. Because of sin which separates us from God, we are destined for an eternity in a terrible place the Bible calls hell.

Thanks be to God; He has not left humanity in this deplorable state. The Bible clearly teaches that because of God's love for all humanity, He has provided a solution to the problem of sin that separates us from Him. What is that solution? Jesus, God's only begotten Son. The Bible says that Jesus paid the price for all sin once and for all on the cross of Calvary. The Bible says in John 3:16 *"For God so loved the world, that He gave His only begotten Son, that whosoever believes in Him shall not perish, but have eternal life."* (NASB)

So now the question is how do we become a child of God? Well, we must accept what Jesus did for us on the cross and believe it by faith. We must confess that we have sinned against Him and receive Christ by faith into our hearts. Then and only then will we become a child of God, having all our sins forgiven. The Bible says, *"But as*

BOB MCLAUGHLIN

many as received Him, to them He gave the right to become children of God, even to those who believe in His name." John 1:12 (NASB)

I believe there are some of you who are reading this passage and right now you want to become a child of God. You want all your sins forgiven and you want the assurance that when you die you will not go to hell but will be ushered into your new home in heaven. Because of this you are now ready to receive Jesus as your Lord and savior.

However, you are not quite sure how to do this. Allow me to help you. All that is required of you at this point is to pray a simple prayer. Prayer is talking with God. If you are ready, and I believe you are, pray this prayer to God. Remember this prayer is from your heart to God.

Pray the following: Dear God, I am a sinner. I have sinned against you. I believe Jesus died for my sins on the cross. I believe He rose from the dead and I want my sins forgiven. I want to be your special child. So right now, I ask Jesus to come into my heart and forgive all my sins. I believe by faith that you now live in me in all your resurrection power. Thank you, Jesus. Amen.

Congratulations my friend! If you just prayed that prayer, a miracle took place in your heart. Jesus has come into you. You have been born again spiritually. You are a child of God, and you have a home in heaven. Yes, you belong to the family of God. Why? Because you just gave Jesus a home in your heart.

If you prayed one of these prayers above, I am so happy for you. You have joined the hundreds of thousands of people who, in our evangelistic campaigns around the world, have repented either by rededicating their lives to Christ or receiving Him for the first time in their lives. Either way you are now on a journey to victory.

It has been my prayer and hope that as you have read this book, you realized and fully understood that God loves you so much that nothing can or does happen to you, good or evil, that God has not

IN THE WAR

allowed for a greater good. Remember, this is the doctrine of meticulous providence.

Remember that no matter what happens to you, God always remains sovereign and is orchestrating your life. Nothing goes unnoticed by Him. He can take all things evil or good and use it for the greater good; His and yours. I pray that you will allow Him now to guide you and place a burden on your heart, a burden that He will fulfill to use you to accomplish His will for your life. He can do amazing things with your life now. Things you never dreamed possible. The Bible says, *"For I am confident of this very thing, that He who began a good work in you will perfect it until the day of Christ Jesus."* Philippians 1:4 (NASB*) "I can do all things through Him who strengthens me."* Philippians 4:13 (NASB).

Having said all this, it is imperative that you take the following critical steps to expedite the process by which you become everything God wants you to become.

First, be sure to find a church that preaches the whole Bible. Church attendance is not optional for the believer. We read in Hebrews 10:25 that we are not to forsake assembling as the body of Christ.

Second, read God's Word, the Bible, daily. This is your spiritual food for growth. The Bible says, *"All Scripture is inspired by God and profitable for teaching, for reproof, for correction, for training in righteousness: so that the man of God may be adequate, equipped for every good work."* 2 Timothy 3: 16-17 (NASB).

Third, pray. Prayer is simply talking with God. The Bible says we are to pray without ceasing. (1 Thessalonians 5:17). This simply means that you can pray at any time. God never sleeps and is always delighted to hear from you. You have access to Him every second of the day. Let your prayer time be filled with praise to Him. If needed, let your prayer time also include confession of any sin, He makes you aware of. The Bible says *"If we confess our sins, He is faithful*

301

to forgive us our sins and to cleanse us from all unrighteousness. "1 John 1:9 (NASB).

Fourth, develop a disciplined life. God gives you the Holy Spirit as a helper. Temptations will abound. However, the Bible says, *"No temptation has overtaken you, but such as is common to man; and God is faithful, who will not allow you to be tempted beyond what you are able, but with the temptation will provide the way of escape also, so that you will be able to endure it."* 1 Corinthians 10:13 (NASB). The Bible also says *"Submit therefore to God. Resist the devil and he will flee from you."* James 1:7 (NASB).

Fifth, be a soul winner. Serve the Lord by sharing the love of Christ with others.

Well, it has been an honor sharing my colorful life with you. And now allow me to bring our time together to a close.

It is imperative that I close with this. In the Bible, we read where Joseph said to his brothers, *"As for you, you meant evil against me, but God meant it for good in order to bring about this present result,..."* Genesis 50:20 (NASB) Undoubtedly, there may be some who read the pages of this book and wonder if they were the ones who were used of the evil one to inflict deliberate pain and cause us trouble. To those of you I humbly tell you that I forgive you. And this may come as a surprise, but I extend to you my thanks as well. Because my God allowed your ill intent to be used of Him to accomplish His glorious will for my life. It is my prayer that you will repent as I have and allow God to help you become all He wants you to become and accomplish all the blessings He has for you. I do love you in the love of the Lord. May God bless each one of you who have ventured to read the entirety of this book. I pray you have been blessed.

In Him and For His Glory,
Bob McLaughlin
Evangelist

Chapter 43

A Word from Bob's Wife

Allow me to share just a little bit about myself. I grew up in a very loving home, so while at home, I felt loved and accepted and secure. However, when I started school, I had a very hard time. I was slower at learning than most of the others in my class and my clothes were not as nice, so I developed an inferiority complex. When I started high school, I found out I could make the kids laugh so I became the class clown. Then I quit school because my boyfriend did, which was not too smart. I know now that one needs to make up their own minds and not follow those who you know are in the wrong.

When I was 17 years old, I got married; when I was 18, I had my first baby; and at the age of 19, I lost my first husband through an accidental death. He was out drinking one night, and it was very cold, so driving onto a side road, he parked his car and left the motor running for warmth and died of carbon monoxide poisoning. When this happened, I felt like the whole world would come crashing down on me.

In time, I met Bob, and when we first met, we were both going through some tough times. We started seeing each other and soon fell in love, but there was a problem. Bob was an alcoholic. I did not want the same thing to happen all over again, so I told him we could not continue a relationship unless he quit drinking. To my great surprise, he did quit drinking and we were married shortly thereafter.

One year after we were married, someone told us the most important news we have ever heard. They told us how much God loves us. He loves us so much that He gave His only Son to die on the cross for our sins, and that if we confess our sins, He is faithful to forgive us our sins. If we ask Jesus to come into our hearts, He will save us from hell, and we would spend eternity in heaven when we die. So, we gave our hearts to Christ and now we know beyond a shadow of a doubt that when we die, we will spend eternity in heaven with our wonderful Savior.

As you have already read in this book, sometimes things happen in our lives that we would never expect. Especially if we let our flesh get in the way and we are not filled and empowered by the Holy Spirit. If we take our eyes off the Lord, we are in trouble. That is what happened to us. When Bob started drinking again, after seventeen and a half years of sobriety, I thought that perhaps he would be able to control his drinking, so I went along with it. At first it was not so bad, but as time went on it got worse, and he started drinking more and more. At first, I felt I should protect him. I was determined to prevent people from discovering his drinking problem. I knew discovery could potentially cost us the ministry. However, as time went on, it got so out of hand that I could no longer handle it.

At the time I was reading in the Old Testament, and it talks about how God used dreams to instruct people as to what He wanted them to do. So I asked the Lord to give me a dream that very night and tell me what I was supposed to do. That very night God gave me the most vivid dream I have ever had. In the dream, God instructed me to leave Bob. I was not instructed to divorce him or even get a legal separation. I was to just leave. In the dream He showed me that I would move in with my daughter and get my own business and soon after I would have my own place.

IN THE WAR

When I awoke from this dream, I knew exactly what I was to do. However, out of pity for Bob, I asked God if we could give Bob one more chance.

I shared my plan with God in prayer as follows: I would move upstairs, and Bob would stay downstairs for one month. If he quit drinking, I would stay. If he continued drinking, I would leave. As it turned out, he did not quit drinking. I had no option at this point. We agreed to call the kids and let them know what was happening and that I was going to leave their dad. They totally understood and even knew this would happen. Well, as it turned out everything that was in that dream came true.

As time went on, I developed deep feelings of bitterness toward Bob. He had really hurt me. A year and a half following our separation, I was visiting a very good friend of mine. She was suffering with rheumatoid arthritis. That day she was having a very bad day. She implied she just wanted to give up on life. Suddenly, I asked her what her favorite number was, she told me the number six was her favorite. I told her my favorite number was seven. I proceeded to tell her that in 2006 she would go into remission and in 2007 Bob and I would get back together. As soon as those words came out of my mouth, I knew it was from the Lord. At this point I started arguing with God, saying there was no way I ever wanted to get back together with him. I could not even stand the thought of reuniting with him. However, as I protested, God just kept telling me over and over to just trust Him. God had a plan for our lives. This all happened one month before Bob quit drinking.

In February of 2005, Bob called me and informed me he had been sober for two weeks and that he was coming home. What came out of my mouth was straight from the Lord because I would not have thought to say what I did. I told him that he was not coming home. I laid down the law. I told him that he must remain sober and continue his involvement with the twelve-step program for two years. I also told him he must remain faithful to me. Also, for the next two years he must be willing to attend professional Christian marriage counselling together with me. I ended my conversation with an ultimatum. If he was willing to comply with my strict guidelines, then, and only then, would I consider reuniting as husband and wife.

To my great surprise, Bob complied with my firm and strict demands. It turned out that upon the completion of the two years, we got back together. Today it is clear to us that our marriage is truly a miracle. We were separated for three and a half years. A miracle indeed.

After being separated for so long, we managed to rebuild our marriage with God's help. I discovered the key to making our marriage a success would have to be forgiveness. God helped me to forgive Bob and gave me the ability to assure him that he is forgiven. Forgiveness for the most part is never easy but necessary if we want to live the way that God wants us to live.

God forgives us of all our sins when we confess them to Him and ask Him to forgive us. If we do, those sins are under the blood of Jesus. Whenever the enemy would remind me of what Bob had done and how he had hurt me, I would talk to the Lord and remember that his sins are under the blood of Jesus, and it is as if he never sinned. I knew Bob had truly repented. So just as God forgave Bob, God forgives me as well. He is faithful to forgive all who ask His forgiveness.

Am I thankful that we are back together? Oh yes! I praise God every day for helping us through this difficult time in our lives. We serve an amazing God, and if we obey Him, He has a wonderful plan for our lives. We love each other more than we had ever loved each other before. He has restored our marriage, our home, our ministry. Praise His Holy Name!

Life still throws difficult things our way, such as the death of our oldest son. The Lord took our Jim home to be with Him. It has been so hard, yet we thank the Lord that Jim rededicated his life back to

IN THE WAR

the Lord before he died of cancer. His dad once told him that we were so sorry he had been inflicted with this terrible cancer, and he replied, "Dad, it is a blessing and therefore the best thing that has ever happened to me because God has given me time to get my life right with Him". It has been nearly 2 years since Jim's passing, and Bob and I still burst out crying when we think about him. The grieving continues.

God answers prayer, so keep praying and don't give up. I also learned that you never know when God is going to take a loved one home. So, say those beautiful words, "I Love You" often and make sure you hug each other. I learned this at a very young age, and I use those words often and hug my loved ones as often as I can.

In closing I pray that you will keep your eyes on the Lord. Obey all that He has for you, you will not regret it. Love the Lord your God with all your heart soul and mind and ask Him daily for wisdom, guidance, and discernment. God Bless You!

Trudy McLaughlin

Author's Readers Guide

The following is a guide of questions and commentary used for personal reflection or thoughtful conversation in a group setting.

1. Throughout this book, the author has repeatedly mentioned the doctrine of "Meticulous Providence." How do you view this doctrine, and does it relate to you personally? If so, do you care to share an event or situation in your life that relates to this?

2. Is there a clear relationship between this doctrine and Romans 8:28?

3. Considering this doctrine, do you think that God causes all the events (good and bad) in the life of a Christian? If your answer is yes or no, can you elaborate?

4. Does the author imply that the Christian is simply being controlled by God, and is nothing more than a "pawn in a spiritual chess game between Satan and God Himself?

5. How could the author have avoided much of the opposition he encountered?

6. How could the author have avoided sliding into the sins that thrust him into a painful crucible and the lose of an international ministry?

7. What are your thoughts regarding the author's account of both angels and demonic encounters, and have you experienced these types of encounters?

8. What are your thoughts regarding God giving instruction to Christians through a dream, as in Trudy's case?

9. Has this book helped you better understand the intense spiritual warfare a person enters once they become a Christian?

10. Has this book helped you personally and if so, how?

11. Would you encourage others to read this book? Why or why not?

We would be interested to receive your opinion about anything related to the contents of this book. You may forward your thoughts and opinions to us via email at b_tmclaughlin@hotmail.com

Author's Bio

Evangelist Evangelist Bob McLaughlin is the founder of Salvation Today Ministries an agency of International Christian Mission Services.

Bob McLaughlin did summer studies conducted by the International School of Theology of San Bernardino, California during his years serving with Campus Crusade for Christ.

He graduated from Briercrest Bible College with a four-year Bachelor of Religious Education degree majoring in "world evangelism."

Evangelist Bob McLaughlin and his wife, Trudy McLaughlin, have been blessed with four children, eighteen grandchildren and one great grandchild.